ROGUE DOCKER

A LIFE OF CRIME IN BIRKENHEAD DOCKS

LEN BURNETT

AMBERLEY

First published 2011

Amberley Publishing
The Hill, Stroud
Gloucestershire, GL5 4ER

www.amberley-books.com

British Library Cataloguing in Publication Data.
A catalogue record for this book is available from the British Library.

ISBN 978 1 4456 0259 2

Typeset in 10pt on 12pt Sabon.
Typesetting and Origination by Amberley Publishing.
Printed in the UK.

This book is intended as a tribute to all the people depicted in its pages and to the many more 'characters' that do not appear in this edition.

No offence is intended to anyone appearing in this edition, and it is hoped that it will be taken as a compliment to all concerned.

Tribute to Men
'on the Docks'

Taken from an interview with P. J. Murphy in *The News*, Wednesday 20 July 1983

When the Mersey Docks & Harbour Company decided to cease cargo handling at Birkenhead, there came to an end a way of life for a breed of men who were as unique as the industry in which they worked – the Birkenhead Docker:

Many are the tales told and the books written about Liverpool and her docks. It was said here stevedores were the best in the world, but most of the cargo handling in Liverpool was discharging – and therefore requiring nowhere the skills of the Birkenhead docker in loading. Above all, Birkenhead was a loading port. Cargoes were bound for the Far East, China and Japan, South Africa, India, Burma and Malaya, and what a cargo it was! It varied from bone china to transformers weighing 200 tons. Not to mention whisky, steam engines, bridges, lorries, cars, bricks, sugar, oil, caustic soda and so on. Transport, laden with goods for all over the world extended for miles around the town.

Each item going into the ship's hold had to be stowed in its own special way. 'Make sure the cargo is checked to ensure it doesn't come adrift at sea. Plenty of timber underneath cases and steel drums to stop the cargo chaffing the bare deck and causing fire. Keep a level at all times, better to work on good ground than ground that looked like a bomb had hit it, and don't over stow, no use putting cargo for Cape Town on top of cargo for Durban if Durban is out first!'

To an 'Easter Bunny', which was the name given to new men who started on the temporary register, the mysteries of stevedoring must have seemed frightening, and so it was that in 1954 at the age of twenty-two, I started work as a docker.

We were hired for work at a control point known as 'The Pen', where we would shape up for the best work we could get. Mostly, we had no choice of our employer and would finish up working hard for a firm that worked no overtime and paid no bonus. This was when the wages were £6.70 a week.

If you worked 'till 7 p.m., four nights a week, this made your money up to £9 – and although the big firms made great profits, this was the time when the ship owners and shareholders enjoyed the fruits of the dockers' labour and when the bonuses paid to the men were so paltry as to be almost non-existent. One could carry two cwt bags of sugar and soda ash all day for a week and be paid a fraction of a penny as a bonus – or lift half-ton drums of octel or caustic at a ship all week for no bonus at all.

It wasn't until the day-to-day tonnage system started in the '60s that the dockers received the bonuses to which they were entitled – and with the closure of 'The Pen' in 1967, and the men being sent to different firms on a permanent basis, things began to get better.

Few tears were shed over that awful place in Corporation Road, where, when work was scarce, one had to push, shove, throw and kick the legs off a man for a job.

If the lifeblood of the Port was the ships, then the men were its heart. There were great characters and personalities – Damon Runyan would have loved them.

There were 'the Prize-fighters', 'the Scholars', 'the Singers' and 'the Entertainers', 'the Penguin', 'the Lemondrop Kid', 'Clear Gums', 'Popeye', 'the Clockwork Mouse', 'the Contented Cat', 'the Quiet Man', 'My Wife's Husband', 'My Mother the Car', 'Scene at 6.30', 'the Werewolf', 'the White Tornado' and 'the Screaming Skull'.

There was Johnny Bee, who would tell of his title fight with Ted Kid Lewis and was ko'd in four rounds because on the day of the fight he was carrying sugar at the Clan – but then proudly proclaimed how he ko'd Tom Berry an Gypsy Daniels.

Then there was Israel Boyle, who had seventy fights and only lost ten and should have been champ, plus Jim Kenny and Big Ozzie. And there was Big Martin, who could – and did – sing everything from music hall to Verdi and Puccini.

Polly Burgess would suddenly burst into Counod's 'Ave Maria' in the middle of the hatch – much to the delight of the men, who would show their appreciation by banging on the bulkhead with their hooks. Then there was Danny O'Leary, who could spin such a fine thread of sound that would do credit to John Macormack.

Lenny Burnett, whose great love for and knowledge of grand opera was revelation, possessed records of every tenor from Caruso to Corelli. Tommy Blood could name and debate on every English monarch from William Conqueror to our present Queen.

Then there were the ships' bosses, like 'The Champ', who would fight any man on the ship after work (bare knuckles, of course) and 'Putty Nose' from Brocks, who demanded and got the best labour in the Port but paid the best wages. It was said if you could stow cargo in the main hatch at Brocks, you were among the greats.

Other employers who ranked among Birkenhead's 'immortals' were Paddy Kieran, whose week of five o'clocks used to break a docker's heart, and 'Cowboy' from the Clan would play a tin whistle.

Ships' managers came and went like ships that passed in the night and yet never played a part in the history of the docks at all. Such were men who preferred a stable deck beneath their feet to the awful sameness of a factory floor or the soul-destroying boredom of a conveyor belt.

With the decline in shipping in the early 1970s, and the coming of containerisation at Seaforth, the days of Birkenhead as a Port were numbered. Anchor and City lines were the first to go and the others were soon to follow.

From billowing smoke to the remains of an abandoned Second World War landing ship tank.

Preface

I must impress upon the reader that it wasn't all about stealing. We worked very hard, most of the time. Some of the conditions we had to put up with would tax any man. But we just got on with it, loading bags by hand which contained cement, sodium chloride, and clouds of dust would go everywhere. This was in the days before we were given gloves and masks. Cases of every weight and description were loaded on board. Sometimes a ship would fill every hold with drums and would take a week to complete. At every level we had to lay planks of wood to enable us to roll the drums in and then head them up (put them upright). This was back-breaking work, and monotonous. Other times it would be heavy, large packing cases, which entailed using blocks and wires to heave them into the wings. Case cars, tractors, sheets of steel plate, pipes of every type, from drain to sewage, iron railway wheels, even the odd railway engine, or even railway lines. This was the magic of such a diversity of cargo that made the job so enjoyable. I cannot say enough about the humour of the men I worked with, despite some of the conditions we worked under. I'll never forget them.

It was the best job in the world.

Since starting this journal, many ex-dockers have passed away and many are mentioned here.

All their names are protected. I have put initials to some, but on the whole they would not have objected. Some were Second World War veterans and a few were younger.

The proud, gleaming hull of *Chirripo* entering dry dock in the 1960s has been replaced today with the rusting hulk of *Sarsia*, which was abandoned twenty years ago.

Glossary of Terms

Working the welt – Eight men in a gang. Split up into two gangs which now means four men in a gang. Four men go to work and the other four absent themselves. Usually for two hours, could be more.

Loot-swag-goodies – The term applies to anything broached from the cargo.

To dress up – This applies to men wrapping yards of cloth around their bodies underneath their own clothes.

Steam – Whisky, gin, vodka, rum, or any other spirits.

Watchmen – Employed by the company to prevent pilfering cargo. Usually well past retiring age. Not very effective. Poorly paid. Long hours. Most were susceptible to a bribe.

Manager – Number one boss of the ship.

Ship's boss – Number two.

Hatch boss – In charge of a hatch.

Stevedore – Docker elected in the gang to tell the others what to do. Used to get a pound extra for the responsibility.

Cage – Enclosed area in the dock shed where all the so-called fine goods were kept prior to going into the ship. Cloth, whisky, tools, personal effects, etc. Protected by steel bars or wire mesh made of toughened steel with the door padlocked. Sometimes a watchman was on duty inside, but not always.

Made up gear – This was usually material ready to wear: suits, shirts, shoes, socks, children's clothes, etc.

Make up – A man sent to a gang to replace a man who is absent.

One off the top – A springboard. Despicable trick by a man not coming back to relieve his mates.

Spar ceiling – General and bagged cargo are kept clear of the ship's side by these lengths of spar ceiling, which are long lengths of timber. Roughly 4 x 1. These rest in cleats bolted to the frames. Usually called stringers. They ran from the deck to the deck-head almost and could be climbed like ladders as they ran fore and aft.

Can hooks – For slinging drums, casks. Also called chine hooks.

Cargo net – A square net of varying size of manila or wire.

Snotter – A length of manila with an eye spliced at each end. Used for slinging.

Riggers – Shore gang who relieve the crew while in port.

Married gear – Two cargo falls shackled together onto the same hook.

Hatch wedge – A piece of hardwood of triangular shape.

General cargo – Consisting of miscellaneous goods carried in small quantities and of varying weight and dimensions, nature, class and condition.

Deck cargo – Goods carried on the open deck.

Chain sling – A length of chain used for working cargo. Usually fitted with a ring at one end and a hook at the other.

Cargo hook – The hook shackled to the end of a fall for loading and discharging cargo.

Cargo fall – Manila or wire rope rove through the head and heel blocks of a derrick and leading to a winch drum. Used for cargo working operations. Also termed a cargo runner.

Bull rope – Rope used when goods or gear have to be dragged.

Portable cargo clusters or arc lights used for night work. Can be lowered by its extension into the hold of a ship to give more light. Usually plugged into a box in the mast-house.

The author on board *Kyra* in 1966.

Rogue Docker

Liverpool Crown Court – 31 March 1976

I stood in the dock looking at the judge's expressionless face. My two partners in crime had just been sentenced to three years' imprisonment each, and had been taken down. Only a few minutes ago they had been keeping me company, but now I was alone except for a warder standing near me. I really didn't know why I was kept waiting. It soon became apparent.

A social worker appeared out of the blue to put in a plea of mitigation on my behalf. I had never seen the man before, but if he could sway the man in the wig, I would be more than happy. But deep down I knew there would be no miracle performed here. After listening attentively for a few minutes, he then turned to me and said, 'I see no reason why I should not send you to prison.' He then sentenced me to three years, and I joined my partners in the cells below.

So ended my career on Birkenhead docks; thirteen years in all. I suppose it had to come sometime, but somehow, you think you can go on forever. I make no excuses for stealing from my employers. But I must impress upon the reader that this was my first and last venture into larceny. I had never taken anything that didn't belong to me before. I had been working down in the holds of many ships for about three years, and seen all manners of pilfering taking place around me. It never bothered me one way or the other to observe it going on. No one ever twisted my arm to help myself. I eventually succumbed to temptation in my own good time. At first I was like the rest of them, taking small items that could fit in your pocket or inside your shirt, in such a way that you hoped the Law didn't think you looked bulky and out of shape. Maybe seven or eight bottles of whisky around your waist kept in place with a belt.

We took whisky, cloth, cigarettes, and toothpaste – anything small enough to get past the Policeman on the gate. I remember one man actually taking out a pressure cooker. But I digress. I soon got bored with playing Russian roulette with small items, and started using my card. We then moved onto large vans and eventually 20-ton trailers to take the stuff away. Also, tractors (two or three at a time), compressors, and steel reels of copper and wire angle iron. All very heavy cargo, but it went.

Trailers were no problem; they were usually left lying around the dock estate and could be picked up at any time. A lot of the cargo I have mentioned which we took away was actually booked onto a ship and would not be missed until it arrived at its destination. I often wondered at the reaction at the other end when they started looking for it.

We even bought a second-hand tractor unit to haul the goods away. Then we would borrow a trailer from somewhere, use it and then dump it. We managed about ten trips with our unit before we lost it to the police. They had it staked out, hoping that we would come and claim it, but we already knew through the grapevine. That was one round we lost, because it was laden with 20 tons of sheet steel.

But it wasn't all stealing on the docks. We worked normally down the hold of the ship, but when the occasion arose we could do the business because of the welt. If the business was going to take longer, we were able to pay men to stay on in our place until we returned. If all this sounds incredible, let me assure you, it is perfectly true. The docks were not like any other industry. I will try and explain the workings as I go along, including hatch bosses, ship's bosses, Managers, working down below in the hold, on the quay, the sheds, floating cranes, and the Pen as it was known in the Sixties. But most of all I'll talk about the men who worked the docks. The men I worked with had the greatest sense of humour in the world; most were hardworking, conscientious and easy-going. Not everyone was a robber. Most took a pride in their ability to stow the cargo safely, despite some appalling conditions in some of the holds – inadequate safety regulations.

Some cargo we handled was not clearly marked. On many occasions we had to touch dirty and very dusty bags containing hazardous substances. Asbestos was handled many times. Protective headgear was very late in coming to the industry. I think it was 1974. Of course, certain official types were supplied with hard hats, but not the men who were in the most dangerous positions – the holdsmen.

I shall never meet men like them ever again, but I shall cherish all the wonderful memories of working with such a great bunch of men.

§

In 1962, I reported for work one morning at 8 a.m. to a small building on the dock road in Birkenhead. I had been sent by the local Labour Exchange with about twenty other men to start a six-week probationary period on the docks. There were no guarantees that we would be kept on, but I wasn't too worried, because I thought it would be a stopgap until I got another job in the haulage business. I had previously been made redundant as a driver, so this would tide me over at the time; or so I thought.

The Pen was situated directly opposite the huge Blue Funnel complex; a 10-foot-high brick wall separated the road from the shipping firms. There were hundreds of acres of storage – huge sheds and berths, and administration buildings. I entered the Pen and was confronted by a few hundred men, standing around talking. Some were reading newspapers; most were smoking. A blue haze floated above them from the many cigarettes, reminding one of the Hiroshima atomic bomb and its mushroom-shaped after-effects. Men would cough and splutter in the smoke-filled atmosphere. There was swearing and laughter going on all around, good-natured banter. Men were heard discussing all sorts of subjects – movies, horseracing, sex, music, the arts, ships that were due, what goods the ships were to carry, pay, who the boss was. You name it, they discussed it.

There were no uniforms; most wore old suits, coats and shirts. Many wore jeans, trousers, boiler suits, jackets, flat caps and woollen hats. Some men had steel hooks slung over their shoulders, although some of the hooks were kept out of sight under a coat, but still positioned over their shoulder. A lot of men didn't have any hooks at all. I soon found out how handy a tool a hook could be when you were down below. Not absolutely necessary, but could save you a lot of hard work or from getting your fingers crushed.

The Pen was more or less square-shaped; on one side near the main entrance was a small office belonging to the Port Labour Officers. Directly opposite on the far wall was where the deckhands would congregate. On the left as you came in were all the holdsmen and Cowards Corner, so called because that is where we all ran to when we didn't want to be hired.

Men were leaning against the nearest wall nonchalantly reading the papers, but I saw a few looking furtively over the top of the office door. There was a lot of shuffling, muttering and milling about. I stood watching the proceedings quietly and waited for something to happen.

Suddenly, I saw a familiar face in the crowd. His name was Dave, but at the docks he was known as 'Springheels'. He filled me in on what was about to happen, so I waited with him. The door to the office opened and the Port Labour Officer came out, accompanied by another man. When people saw this other man, there was a mad rush to get away.

I asked Springheels why; he snarled, 'Keep away from that prick; he'll give you a week of five o'clocks and a broken back in the bargain.' I didn't have a clue what he meant, but when in Rome. We made ourselves scarce and tried to burrow into the crowd packed in Cowards Corner. Now I knew why it was called the Pen – men milling about just like sheep, but that's where the comparison ends. If you picked your feet up, you would be borne along with the crowd; it was packed tight. It was kind of exciting in a way. You would think the men were about to face a firing squad. When a man was collared for work, the look on his face was a sight to see as he handed over his book. Eventually, enough men were selected and they would leave the Pen.

The men left then relaxed and were able to breathe a lot easier. But it wouldn't last long, because the office door would soon open again. All eyes were focused on that door. I wouldn't have been surprised to see Dr Mengele come out, such was the look on the faces around me. Again, the Port Labour Officer came out, followed by another man. It appeared that this other man was from the Clan Line looking for labourers, but still, some men did not want to go; so they burrowed their way through the crowds to hide. But there was no escaping the Labour Officer; he would just barge into the crowd and it would part like the Red Sea for Moses. The escapees would be exposed like newborn babes on the wall; sickly grins greeted the Labour Officer, who just held out his hand for their books, which they handed over reluctantly. Springheels told me we'd better make a move, so we offered our books, which were taken.

In all, about five gangs were hired for this particular ship starting that morning.

So I had been hired to go to work on my first ship as a docker. I was to work on a tramp steamer that took me around the world in fourteen months. I was mildly excited at the prospect of actually working in a ship's hold loading the cargo on board. About three gangs, including myself and Springheels, started the five-minute walk from the Pen to the *Clan Macgillivray*, berthed at Vittoria Dock. It was now about half past eight in the morning, and we were in no hurry to get there. Turning left at the dock gate, we passed the Blue Funnel berth and over the swing bridge, and into the Clan Line sheds.

The *Macgillivray* was high out of the water, and there was a big gangway leading down from her main deck to the shed floor. The shed was similar to a huge airplane hangar, with cargo piled high like miniature skyscrapers, and more was coming all the time. Cases littered the floor, pipes, bags, reels of wire, huge drums of copper wire, cardboard boxes, all piled high in the air. Blue stencilled letters denoted the port of destination – Mombasa, Aden, Dar es Salaam, Djibouti, Port Louis, and Mauritius. These were just some of the ports of call. Mobile cranes and stacker trucks were scurrying all over the place, smoke belching from their exhausts. Men were shouting, lorry drivers rushing about with bundles of shipping notes in their grubby hands, looking for a checker to get their loads discharged quickly. Not much chance of that so early in the day; he'd be in the dockside canteen getting his tea and toast. Outside, the shed railway wagons were being shunted, warnings shouted to the unwary. Traffic was coming into the sheds continuously, horns blaring, adding to the confusion. Even the roosting pigeons high up on the girders fled the scene for a while, until things calmed down a little. The exhaust fumes rose up to reach even them, who thought they were safe. Sometimes a docker would be the target for one of those birds, who didn't care where it dropped its business. This would give the lads a good laugh.

I saw a mobile crane dragging a bundle of steel rods along the deck with the jib lowered, sometimes the crane tilted, with the rear wheels lifting slightly. The driver would stop, wait for the wheels to touch the ground again, and start dragging once more. I didn't envy their job; eyes were needed in the back of their heads. A slightly built chap went past dragging two long sweep wires. I heard a voice behind me snarl, 'Look at that prick, Nobby. He's not even at this ship, but he's pinching our fucking wires.' Nobby saw us and grinned, and gave us a 'V' sign. Nobby looked like Nick Cravat, Burt Lancaster's sidekick in *The Crimson Pirate*.

One had to keep one eye on the pigeons above and keep out of their line of fire and also keep out of the way of the bustling traffic all around. We stood at the bottom of the shed in a mob.

Most were smoking and making sure they weren't caught by a strolling dock policeman because it was strictly forbidden to smoke in the shed. Men were sorting themselves out as to who they were going to work with.

'Don't get with that fuckin' glassback; it's like workin' a man out … couldn't pull you out of bed,' said one man, referring to a small, slightly built docker with glasses.

'Should have been a deckhand; he's fuckin' useless down below,' said another voice sarcastically.

Some quayhands came up dragging ropes.

'Where did he say that fuckin' cargo was for? Lourenço Marques?' said a burly docker with a red face and cheese-cutter hat.

His mate, a smaller man with a face like a weasel, replied, 'Said it was over here behind the Port Said cargo, but I can't fuckin' see it anywhere.'

'He said it's clearly marked,' said the burly man.

'So where the fuck is it?'

Just then a man wandered in carrying a pot of blue water paint and a brush. They watched him disappear into a huge mound of cases. After a few minutes he came out.

'Worruvya just marked la?' asked the Weasel.

'Larry Marks,' said the painter.

'How the fuckin' hell are we gonna get at that behind that lot?' asked the burly man angrily.

His mate just shrugged his shoulders. 'Don't ask me. If it's in there we have to gerrit.'

The burly docker looked frustrated. 'You make a start. I'll go and get the fuckin' crane.'

We all watched this little carry-on with great amusement. Another docker chipped in with 'Those two are better than Laurel and Hardy.'

'I wonder who's doin' the ship?' asked another, meaning who was the ship's boss. Just then Les Noonan was seen walking down the shed accompanied by a timekeeper. This is where I found out all about the welt and its workings. He finally reached us and looked at the crowd of us milling around. The timekeeper got his clipboard ready to take the numbers as each man gave it to him. I still stuck by Springheels, and waited to see what he would do next.

He had warned me about the piss artists and glassbacks. These were some of the men to avoid working with. The former couldn't make it through the day without a drink; very unreliable and would sometimes leave you on all afternoon. The latter would, and could, cause you a lot of back trouble, because they couldn't (or wouldn't) put their weight or strength behind a case to help you turn it over. If you all pulled together, it would be no problem, but one weak link could cause trouble.

'Right lads, got yourselves sorted? Then let's have eight holdsmen out here,' called out Les Noonan. I walked out with Dave and six others, and we gave our numbers to the timekeeper. We were the first to be hired and were to go down number two hatch. After this formality, we moved away from the hire to sort ourselves out into two gangs, and tossed a coin to see who was going aboard to start the job, or going for breakfast. Dave and I made up one gang and lost the toss, so we had to go on the ship. Whilst we were doing this, we had to make sure the boss didn't see us, as the welt was unofficial. Also, we had to make sure he didn't see the other gang slipping away to the canteen, or wherever they were going. Once the boss had asked for holdsmen, he then asked for deckhands and quayhands; even those people worked the welt. I was highly amused at what was going on around me. It was quite ridiculous really; we had just been hired to work and already we had tossed to see who didn't. So we were on till 10 a.m., and when the other four came back we were off until 1 p.m. That was three hours where we were absent from the job, but, as they say, 'When in Rome'. Also, I might add that each gang tossed up to see who would be the Stevedore and 'had' the bar. This was a steel bar used down below to assist in stowing the cargo; used as a lever, it came in very handy. It was about 4 feet long, curved at one end, and pointed at the other. It had other uses, such as forcing padlocks on cage doors, or opening wooden cases bound with steel bands. I think the Stevedore in each gang was awarded an extra pound a week for the responsibility. A lot of men shied away from this. But generally we all got stuck in and helped each other in stowing the cargo, and anyone could use the bar if they wanted to. The reason some didn't was in case anything went wrong; for example, if a case was damaged or the cargo stowed in the wrong place, the Stevedore would take all the flak. Which was nothing really, because we would tell whoever was complaining to fuck off, or threaten to walk off the ship, and that would work like magic.

I soon merged into the way of life on the docks. The welt was an accepted fact. But you had to use common sense. For example, you just couldn't walk off the ship if the Manager happened to be standing near the gangway, or perhaps on the quay. Discretion had to be used. It was much safer to wait until he had gone, or had turned his back. Even then you had to move fast. If he saw you, you had no alternative but to go back to your job, otherwise he would get the timekeeper and go around the hatches to find out who was missing. There were bound to be men missing from each hatch. Some men just wouldn't listen to reason and would go barging past the Manager as if they had every right to. That was just like adding insult to injury. They thought the welt was their divine right, but of course it wasn't.

For a few years we used the old Pen until a new complex was built on the dock estate, a few yards from the Clan Line sheds. What a difference. Bright and airy, plenty of windows. A two-storey building. Upstairs were rows of steel lockers with wooden benches between. Showers were available too. The ground floor was equipped with tables and chairs for the men to sit at while waiting to be hired.

Vending machines stood at one end dispensing tea, coffee, soup, even hot chocolate. The other end was a large office. The hiring was done through a tannoy system by the PLO from within this office. Gone were the days of Cowards Corner and running around the pen like sheep. Instead, everything was civilised and orderly. By this time, I was no longer an Easter Bunny. One of the first things I learned was to get some sort of transport. It wasn't essential, but it was handy. There was a fair amount of walking to do sometimes when you were hired. For instance, you may have had to get to the Bidston Dock, or even Lewis's Quay. Most of the lads used to take a leisurely stroll to the ship. A bike was handy if you didn't live too far and you were going home for dinner; sometimes you could get held up by one of the many bridges on the dock estate, and if you had transport you could perhaps take another route through the sheds and out another gate. It sure did save a lot of walking. Those were my Russian roulette days when I had a bike. I soon learned the danger zones. Some berths were considered fairly safe if you were carrying off a ship, and others were taboo. But it all really came down to pure luck.

Sometimes, when we first went aboard a ship that was just starting, we might find the hatches battened down but the derricks raised. We would take off the two or three tarpaulins, folding them up and placing them on the main deck. Then the hatch-boards had to be taken off and stacked next to the hatch. On the more modern ships that came later, they had MacGregor-type hatches; these were steel lids that were jointed and were lifted up using a wire runner. This took about five minutes. Simpler and easier than conventional wooden hatch-boards. With hatch-boards you had to shift steel beams and these were usually dragged forward or aft and secured. This wasn't always easy. Some seemed to be welded in place and had to be hit forcefully to dislodge them. This meant using a hatch-board as a battering ram, or asking the crane driver to swing the heavy iron ball on the end of his fall to do the same. This was only because the crew didn't keep the channels oiled and cleaned. The odd beam would get knocked completely out of the channel and go hurtling down, usually gouging a hole in the wooden deck. If there was part cargo down there it was just too bad. Sometimes a ship's officer would be present on some occasions and start foaming at the mouth about the damage, whereupon some comedian present would come out with, 'Don't fuckin' worry. Worse things have happened at sea …' But this always seemed to infuriate him more. We always seemed to find times like this funny. Maybe someone would pass a remark like, 'Get the lazy fuckin' crew out and grease the fuckin' channels.' Of course, this wouldn't go down too well with the Mate. Another hazard was trying to pull the beams up hill if the ship had cargo at one end or the other. For example, if there was cargo in the after hatch, the forepart would be raised slightly, thus making it extremely difficult for us. But we did it with good humour like everything else. Now and again they would do us a favour and send the beams ashore and place them on the quay, because the decks would be strewn with debris, clusters, hatch-boards, ventilators, and sometimes deck cargo and ropes. Once the hatch was stripped we would have to get below. There were two ways you could do this. Throw your leg over the coaming and climb down the steel ladder, which was welded or bolted, or go down the trunkway in the mast-house. These were nearly always in total darkness, so you had to feel your way down. You might collect a few bumps and bruises during this descent.

Stripping a batch was fairly easy in the summer. When the winter came it brought a few problems. There would be snow on the deck, and there could be ice underneath, or oil. Ringbolts would be hidden of course, and you could find yourself caught off balance. Deckhands would be trying to set their derricks. Preventer wires that were covered in oil could catch you in the face if you weren't quick enough to duck; pulley blocks would be swinging all over the place as the derricks were being swung into position. You had to be alert at all times when this operation was being carried out. Especially if they were raising or lowering the derricks, one would be on the drum end watching the turns, and another might be making sure the topping life was free of kinks. I remember a man losing a foot just above the ankle because the man at the drum end lost control and the turns flew off, which caused the derricks to crash down just missing another man who was looking down the hatch. Another man lost both legs in a horrific accident, again caused by a wire. The docks could be a very dangerous place to work sometimes. There used to be a television programme called *The Naked City*, and they always said, 'There are a million stories.' Well, the same applied to the docks, and I shall try and remember some of them.

§

I watched men stealing for about three years before I succumbed. I remember 'The Crab', because he seemed to walk sideways, stuffing his pockets with tubes of toothpaste to take off the ship. He offered to help me but I declined. I thought it was stupid to lose your book because of petty theft. But as I have said, I started doing the same thing. I still think it was stupid to do so. But I later got greedy and ambitious. It was all down to nerve really; you were playing with fire when you did such stupid things. But they did it, so why not? Walking past a policeman on the gate when laden with stolen goods took some nerve. A matter of time before you got pulled in for a search. A gang of men could be going out and the policeman would take someone at random. You had to make sure your face didn't give you away if you were carrying. If stopped, you could always run for it, but it would be difficult if you had seven or eight bottles of whisky stuffed down your trousers, or twenty yards of cloth wrapped around your body.

If you were attempting to carry goods from any ship – stolen goods that is – hoping to get past the police on the gate, you had to make sure you did not look too bulky. Also you had to possess a little bottle, and if possible try not to look guilty. I have seen men throwing up before leaving the ship. I asked one man not to do it if he felt apprehensive about trying. It's not worth losing your book for. But most of them went ahead anyway. I knew one man who was approached by a policeman about to stop him and search him. He was walking through the shed at the time. He ran away and dumped his loot without the policeman seeing him. The well-known policeman asked him why he had run away. He explained he thought he was about to be attacked. The policeman was in plain clothes and knew the docker was taking the piss.

You would get the odd man who couldn't handle the situation when caught and would throw his hand in and even confess to the acid bath murders … Even without the pilfering on the docks, it was the best job in the world. I could never imagine punching a time clock in a factory on a regular basis.

§

When I first started on the docks, we worked from 8 a.m. till 7 p.m. Quite a long day, but with the welt it was much easier. When the new scheme was introduced, everyone was much happier. We only worked four hours out of eight. It was great to leave the ship at 3 p.m., and go home finished for the day. But the next day you had to stay on until 5 p.m., but still, it wasn't so bad. Anything was better than a 7 p.m. finish.

I know it sounds ridiculous, but that was the way it was on the docks. Some men worked the half a day about, sometimes the whole day. I never fancied that myself, I thought it was asking for too much trouble. You could come unstuck quite easily if the job changed. For instance, you could be having it easy with four men coping well enough, but then it could change suddenly and you would find the work piling up on the quay and then the hatch boss would start snarling at the holdup down below. Management would look the other way while the welt was being worked, but let there be a holdup anywhere and all hell would break loose. This is where the trouble started.

The boss would come down the hatch and want to know where the other four men were. He would arrive on the scene and send for the timekeeper, and then they would check all the hatches. There would be men absent from these as well. Sometimes the lads would leave their phone numbers so they could be contacted at home, or even the number of a local boozer. Some would come back quickly, but some were full of ale and wouldn't budge. 'Ah, fuck it, we're not moving ...' and they would remain in the boozer until closing time. I jumped in my car once and tried to get some of the lads to get back to the ship with me from a pub, but was told to fuck off! With that sort of attitude you had no chance. So they would go on report, and lose half a day's pay. Any other job in the world and you would be fired immediately, and rightly so. But the docks were like no other industry anywhere; you could get away with murder – almost.

When you were working in the lower hold, you had the lower tween deck to protect you from the cargo coming in on a crane or winch. It had been known for cargo entering the ship to tip up and hurtle down and smash on the deck. Bags, cases, drums, every conceivable commodity was exported. Even lengths of tubular piping of all sizes were brought on board. I remember one such sling breaking in mid-air, and all their missiles flying all over the hatch like arrows at Agincourt. Men were breaking land speed records to get out of the way. Never had I seen so many budding Tarzans leaping for the stringers, striving for height and safety. We would really laugh at times like that; I suppose it was a safety release on our part. No one ever wore a safety helmet, simply because they were not even thought of. They wouldn't have been much use anyway. Not much protection against a hundredweight at least. Or a 50-ton locomotive. The least you could hope for was a broken limb. I remember J.D. walking out from the protection of the tween deck to make up a rope sling, and a hundredweight drum smashed into the deck a foot away from him. It had fallen off a pallet board. If it had hit him that would have been it. You had to think all the time never to walk out into the hatch when cargo was coming in. But you sometimes forgot the danger and did something stupid. Most times you got away with it (though not always), just getting a mouthful of abuse from the deckhand doubting you had a father and sense. Of course, you had to accept it all.

You had to have eyes in the back of your head, especially if you had a stacker truck working with you. Nasty if one of them ran over your feet, so steel toecaps were essential. If you didn't get run over, you could get impaled on the forks, or if one came off altogether, it would break a bone easily. He only had to run over a bit of timber to shake one free. I think this is where a lot of dockers had their first driving lesson, because everyone had a go at them. No tax, no insurance, no licence required, and no other vehicle to hit, only your mates if they were soft enough to stand around. If the driver wanted to go for his beer and we had a good job, one of us would take over for a while. If we didn't like him, he had no chance.

The stacker made life a lot easier for us down below, but it wasn't like that all the time. Most of the time we had to handball all the cargo in, using the passing gang method; that's if the cargo was small enough.

Sometimes when you were up the stringers with a gall wire in one hand and holding on with the other, there was no place to secure the gall wire. No ringbolt, no little crevice between the deck-head and the cross member. There might be one further away from where you needed to put it, so you had to get a longer wire and reeve this through, and then reeve your gall wire through it. It was most difficult when you were hanging on with one leg over the stringer and holding a steel block. When you're heaving in, there is a terrific amount of strain on the wire, so there must be no sharp edges to snap the wire holding the block. But it didn't always work out that way; in fact, it was impossible sometimes. So we just did our best in the circumstances and kept clear. If we couldn't get the wire out after we had finished, we just left it. To make it easier when there was no ringbolt or hole to get a wire through, we sometimes used another block called a clamp. This was taken aloft and clamped to a cross member over the place where you would normally have a ringbolt. Here again there were problems. The clamp would slide along the member under pressure, so a piece of wood had to be jammed into it so that it wouldn't. There was a fixture in the clamp to enable you to shackle your block to it. It was satisfying after all this preparation to see a large case land exactly where you wanted it. Just the right amount of heaving and expert hand signals to the deckhand made everything that much easier.

Getting large cases on top of some others was another work of art that called for teamwork. If you had a stacker truck down below with you that would help considerably. Sometimes the stacker driver did things that he wasn't supposed to. It could get very dangerous during these operations, but most of them never complained; they just got on with it. Some modern ships are so designed that there is no tween decks and the cargo is lowered into the hold, placed against the ship's side and that's it. So much easier than all the messing about with blocks, wires, battens, gall wires, clamps. But how boring. But that's progress, I suppose. Incidentally, I forgot to mention that sometimes those ringbolts that were welded to the bulkhead got ripped right off by the pressure on them. When you worked similar cargo in the after hatches, which sometimes you did, you had to contend with the tunnel shaft. This was a protective covering for the propeller shaft that came from the engine room, through No. 4 and No. 5 hatch usually. I've seen plenty of these battered and bent through being hit over the years by cargo, and by the huge 20-ton steel grabs if she had been carrying bulk cargo such as sulphur, coal, phosphate, pyrites, etc.

§

The work was not always demanding – sometimes it was easy. You never knew what was coming in. Heavy cases, not-so-heavy cases, bales, cartons, drums, bags, steel plate, reels of wire, cement, pipes of every description, underground sewer pipes, drainage, etc. If a few tons of bags were coming in we would place two wooden tubs, one on top of the other to land the sling of bags on just to make it easier for us to pick up from waist high instead of picking them up from the deck. This would be backbreaking work. You still had to carry the bags maybe a hundred yards, and as you filled up the space, it was less and less to walk back to the landing site.

Don't forget at the same time there would be burst bags, so there would be clouds of dust everywhere and in a confined space it could be rather stifling. Not so bad in winter but summer a lot worse. But we still had our sense of humour no matter what.

We could walk into an empty shed and in the next hour there would be bedlam. Vehicles would be coming in one after the other. This is where one had to be very watchful. Stackers would be flying around, cranes also. Horns would be blowing, clouds of exhaust fumes would be adding to the confusion. Checkers would be walking around looking for a certain vehicle to chuck his load and deciding where it was to be offloaded in the shed. They would all be jockeying for position. The head of security would be there keeping an eye on any vehicles carrying whisky or fine goods which were kept in a special enclosure they called a cage consisting of steel wire mesh and they would put a watchman in there, usually past retiring age and were paid a pittance A few of them would look the other way if we decided to raid it.

J.D. and I were in a position to have stuff placed where we could get at it later. Also if we wanted to get at the whisky or gin, bacardi, rum, etc., we would place cases against the cage fence and arrange a sort of tunnel where we could go to work with a hacksaw making just enough room to crawl through and pass cases out. It was hard work sawing through the steel mesh, but the rewards were worth it. But we still had to get it out of the dock gate, and there was usually a policeman on duty. Plus we had to make sure the watchman didn't hear us.

§

Deep tanks were used for water or fuel, sometimes cargo. Situated at the bottom of the hatch with huge, square, steel lids or covers. There could be as many as twenty or thirty bolts holding them down, and of course these all had to be unscrewed. In the Blue Funnel, they used these tanks for liquid latex, coconut oil or palm oil, or general cargo. Once you were down below in one of these tanks there was no escape if any dusty bags burst on the rim of the tank. It all depended on the judgement of the deckhand passing the word. If he was full of booze, God help you. It could be worse; he could throw up. It happened many times.

Most deckhands were hard-working and conscientious and did their best. When any bags burst, there would be a frantic race for the steel ladder to get out quickly. Just imagine four men trying to get up all at the same time. It was hilarious sometimes. Some of the bags were unmarked, so they could have contained poisonous substances for all we knew, so the best thing was to get out of the way quickly and try and hold your breath until you got clear. An amusing incident happened once at Lewis's Quay at a Clan ship. We were working down a tank. We were about six or seven feet from the top. I had just got out of the tank to watch Dave the Queer throwing some slabs down to use after dinner, as it was just coming up to dinnertime. Somehow, a misshaped length of wood caught in his clothing and he fell into the tank, dragged by the wood. As it happened, we were loading bag-ash and this is what saved him from serious injury. He managed to fall onto his back, and he lay there stunned. I immediately jumped down to assist him. He tried to get up right away, but I advised him to stay down and take a long count. He was sent out in a tub. Of course, he needed witnesses to put a claim in right away. He promised me and another guy a small reward. I personally did not want a cent, but the fall seemed to have affected his memory anyway, because he did get some money, we heard, but nothing came our way. He was a nice enough chap to work with but slightly eccentric.

Another deep tank I remember was with Mr B. loading fine goods but the watchman was a bastard. He wasn't down the tank fortunately, so I stayed down one dinner hour. Mr B. put the lid on to kid him. I had a torch, so I got some stuff ready to carry off for myself and Mr B. We did manage to get something out of it anyway.

Another place we had to work was in steel lockers. These were situated in some of the hatches. They stretched across the hatch from one side to the other and had a door that could be padlocked. Anything would be stowed in here. Fine goods, whisky, or even general cargo. The worst cargo was dusty bags. You had to wear a mask inside these places because the dust was everywhere. The slings were landed on a tub so you could grab your bag without bending down to the floor. Then you had to walk in quite a way, but as you slowly filled the locker up, the nearer you got to the door and, of course, the easier the job became. We were always glad to get out of these places. When the whisky was stowed in these lockers, they usually had a watchman inside with you to make sure you didn't help yourself. Sometimes they even had a young apprentice officer there as well to keep an eye on things. But if he liked a drink that made things easier for us. I have been in a locker with two watchmen and still managed to get a few bottles. Always hairy climbing the ladder out of the hatch carrying battles of whisky in your belt; you had to be very careful when you threw your leg over the coaming to reach the main deck. There was usually a watchman on the deck as well to watch the pallet boards leave the quay and go straight down the hatch without stopping for someone to help themselves to a few cases. It's all a matter of timing really. If the watchman didn't watch the board go down the hatch, the crane driver would stop at the tween deck and someone there would grab a few cases quickly and hide them. Then the board would carry on down. This could only happen if no one was looking up from the bottom of the hatch. You had to watch out for crew members hanging around who would run to the Mate and snitch on you. Your eyes had to be everywhere to make sure no one was watching you. It didn't always go your way though, but you had to make the best of everything. Some you won, some you didn't. You can't win all the time. But I still got upset if things didn't go right for me. But I always believed in the old maxim, 'Who dares, wins ...' Sometimes a ship would come around the land. This meant it could have come from Cardiff, Swansea, Glasgow, or any other big port. We would go down the hatch and see cargo that had been stowed by those other chaps. Particularly from Glasgow was the whisky. We would find the locker full of it but padlocked. That was the biggest laugh. We would use a hacksaw to get it off and then replace it with one of our own. Unless the Security was very sharp they wouldn't notice the switch.

One particular watchman at the Clan was rather keen, and was very observant. This was Mr S. He was in charge of security and did not trust any docker at all. J.D. and I waged a battle of wits with him, and I like to think he had a few nightmares at our antics. He knew we were at it. Sometimes I felt quite sorry for him because he was only doing his job. But all is fair in love and war. Getting back to the lockers: they were usually made of steel with a couple of ventilators at the very top, covered by thick mesh wire. Not big enough for a man to crawl through, but there were ways and means to get at the whisky if you were determined enough, and we always were – always. This mesh could be ripped out, or cut, and then you could reach in as far as possible to get the bottles. And when they were out of reach with an arm, then you used wire, or the bar, to get further bottles. I have seen men standing on someone's shoulders trying to get them. We could fill one of these lockers up and get absolutely nothing at all; that's the way it went.

The easiest locker I ever encountered was in a Clan ship, and it was full of different brands of whisky. I just couldn't believe my eyes; it was so vulnerable. We made a killing with this particular locker, but more about that later.

§

I must stress that it wasn't all stealing. We still had to work and very hard too, sometimes. The welt made everyone a lot happier, but it was still a restrictive practice. But we all took our chances of being caught away from the job. Birkenhead was a loading berth, and in fourteen years working there, I only ever saw about half a dozen ships being discharged. Even then it was usually a few hundred tons, except at Rea's Wharf where they discharged a lot more, but that was mainly steel billets, or paper, etc. The only ship I worked on discharging cargo in Birkenhead was a rusty old Liberty-type steamer called *Whitehorse*. We discharged a few hundred tons of asbestos, without gloves or masks I might add. The Leper and Andy the Liar cursed me for jumping out for this ship and dragging them with me. But it wasn't that bad a job. From 1963 until the early 1970s, I used to take photos of these old American-built steamers of Second World War vintage. I went aboard about 140. I saw the last one in 1971. What a shipbuilding programme that was in the United States. Well over 2,700 built. Mainly prefabricated and welded. They proved themselves time and time again, tramping all over the world at ten knots.

In the Sixties, Birkenhead docks were extremely busy. The quays and avenues were always congested with lorries, trains, vans, all trying to get their loads discharged. Even outside the dock, in the roads leading to the docks, were lines of lorries parked up, all waiting to get in. The drivers used to spend the night in their cabs, or in one of the many lodging houses in the area. It was the same in Liverpool. The dock road was one continuous line of vehicles and plenty of carthorse transport, patiently waiting. Horses with their nosebags on, lifting their heads to get at the grain or straw at the bottom or lifting a leg to clatter their hooves on the cobblestones. Of course, Liverpool was much bigger than Birkenhead docks – miles and miles of docks and a much bigger workforce. At that time you could go along the dock road and see all the famous funnels: Blue Star, T&J Harrison, Brocklebank, CPR, Cunard, Royal Mail, Elder Dempster, NZSC, MacAndrews, Palm Line, and many, many more. And of course there were plenty of foreign flagships or tramps flying the flag of Costa Rica, Panama, Liberia, Greece, and many more. Maybe in the river there would be other ships swinging on the hook such as *Baron Geddes*, *Sycamore Hill*, *Amberton*, *Pikepool*, *Ericbank*, and the ships of the Headlam Line, *Sneaton* and *Sandsend*. There could be ships waiting to get up to Ellesmere Port with sulphur, pulp, or grain. Now the river is empty.

I went aboard the *Sneaton* when she was in Birkenhead discharging grain. I saw her builder's plate lying on the steel grating over the engine room. I regret not taking it because she went for scrap later, but I consoled myself because I already had four other builder's plates, which I had taken from other Liberty ships. I think she was originally the *Samstrae*. Certain dockers were on call to work the grain ships. They could be working down below with you and suddenly get called to one. Working the grain was easy when you were sinking. But when you got further down, you had to start using what they called the Plough. This piece of fiendish equipment was dragged through the grain with you behind it, trying to steer it. It was very dusty work and I am glad to say I only went once to a grain ship. No thanks.

In the late Sixties, I heard a rumour that the docks in Birkenhead were going to be filled in. At that time I did not think such a thing possible, the whole concept was completely ludicrous. But as events proved later, someone knew it was going to happen.

A lot of us did eventually begin to accept that something was happening when the volume of shipping began dropping off in the early Seventies. We started to sign on more because there were fewer ships in. Then severance pay was offered and some of the men accepted it and left the industry. Each year the severance went higher and more left. I suppose £16,000 looked very tempting. I thought then that it just wasn't worth selling your job for that amount. At the time of writing, I believe it is now over £30,000. A great improvement, I think. Especially if you are near retiring age, or in bad health. But I know several dockers who bitterly regret ever accepting the severance pay, but I suppose you live and learn. A lot blew their cash quickly on booze, helped by the usual freeloaders. A pity some of them didn't seek expert advice while they still had their money, but some of them wouldn't have listened anyway.

I have left out a great deal of certain schemes and wildcat strikes that occurred during my time on the docks. To be honest, I cannot remember what half of the strikes were about. Most of them were stupid. They got so bad, we got labelled 'Garrisons Guerillas' at the Clan Line, because we would strike at any time. A pamphlet came out in 1963 with a grandiose title: *A new deal for Merseyside registered dockworkers*. The only snag was we had not been consulted about it. In it was a plan for four grades of employees, which included a 10 per cent pool of casual workers. It was rejected by everyone as a new slavery system. But in 1967, after the Devlin report, things began to improve. Decasualisation arrived and we went on strike for six weeks. A great start. A port workers' committee was set up and tried to get us back to work, but we would not consider it until the employers agreed to a more favourable agreement. After all, the piecework on London docks was four times higher than ours. Also they were to abolish the welt. Mr Jack Scamp and his Inquiry agreed with the dockers, who up until then had to work excessive overtime for a decent living wage. We eventually agreed to work the new system. We were guaranteed a basic £17 for a forty-hour week, with a fallback wage of £15. We were all allotted different firms to work for but could be sent out to another one if required. So for the time being we were fairly happy with the arrangement, plus the welt still existed, but you had to be very careful how you worked it. It was still a restrictive practice.

During this time, negotiations got under way for a better deal for handling dangerous and dirty cargo. We also appointed shop stewards for the very first time. In 1971, shift work was reduced to fall in line with the Devlin Inquiry. Daytime shift was from 8 a.m. to 6 p.m. with a one-hour break. The mini shift was from 5 p.m. to 11 p.m. And the night shift was from 11 p.m. to 6 a.m. Ten per cent of dock workers were leaving each year, accepting severance pay somewhere around £1,800. But this was only if you were in poor health and had worked for at least twenty-five years. Later, the money went up to £2,300. Later, higher severance pay was promised, and a lot of men began thinking of leaving.

The writing was on the wall. Ships that had been seen in the docks for over sixty years began to disappear. It was unbelievable that the

Clan Line would go. City would follow. Blue Funnel also. You had to believe it then. Even now, as I write, when I go past Birkenhead docks, I see the sheds with a few laid-up ships moored alongside. Not a sign of the once-familiar funnels.

§

When you were hired for night work you started at 11 p.m. and finished at 7 a.m., but you still worked the welt. The good thing about nights was the fact that you could have a few hours' sleep during the day then go out somewhere, take in a movie, do some decorating on the house. You could get your head down on the ship during the night, if you could find somewhere warm, especially in the winter. In the Indians' mess room aft on the Clan ships if you could find a vacant seat at any of the tables or in the alleyways. The mess room would smell like a Lebanese brothel – cigarette smoke, the overpowering smell of curry, men would be breaking wind left, right and centre, making tea at the urn over the sink. The heat would be intense with all the men crowded into the small mess room. Bodies would be lying in the alleyways trying to sleep, risking a kick in the head from the many feet stepping over them. Now and then an old Indian seaman would creep out of his cabin aft and try and get into the mess room to make his tea and then creep back. I should mention that next door to the mess room were the Indians' toilets. The smell from this place would make you heave, but no one complained in the winter when the snow and ice was on the decks. Sometimes men would try to get into the engine room. You could get your head down on the steel gratings unless some fussy engine rating on duty gave you the bum's rush, which he had every right to do. Pity, because it was the warmest place on the ship.

Sometimes the lads would get very noisy over something and start arguing. This would start the crew members complaining (and rightly so). If you were on nights with Danny Kaye (alias the Leper), he would make certain you didn't sleep. People groaned when they saw him coming and would reach for the headache pills. He was an expert on boxing, movies, knew all the Oscar winners, and knew most of the capital cities of the world. When in his company you got no peace. You thought you had left your school days behind until you worked with him. He never gave up. If you didn't know anything, by the time the ship finished you would have a degree in English, history, geography, spelling, movies and boxing. Millions of general knowledge questions would be hurled at you with the speed of a bullet. There was never a dull moment with him, and if you were on nights with him, God help you. He would dare anyone to ask him questions on any subject, especially boxing. Someone would always rise to the bait. 'Here's one you don't know ...' but the Leper always beat them. This infuriated some men and then you would hear the famous words, 'How much do you wanna bet?' When money was mentioned, some men had a change of heart. On a few occasions, I urged the Leper to take their money, but he would never take it off them. A bet is a bet. You lose, you pay up. Some people you could never win a round with because in their eyes they were always right. Laughable really, but that is what it was like on the docks. There were quite a lot of men who knew quite a lot about a specialist subject: royalty, movies, birds, pop music, the Second World War, all sorts of music, the arts, painting, opera. Some men didn't communicate as well as others – not that they weren't gregarious; some were naturally quiet, a few almost shy.

Getting back to being off welt aft in the Indian mess room, the hot air blowers would be going full blast adding more heat to the already humid mess room. Men would be snoring, stirring tea, cursing, coughing, cigarette smoke would be thick in the air. Men would be eating, drinking tea, and trying to talk at the same time. Butties of every description – bacon, salmon, jam, corned beef, marmalade. Dessert would consist of canned pears or pineapple rings taken from the hatch cargo, chocolate biscuits, shortbread. Sometimes it was just like feeding time at the zoo. There might even be whisky getting passed around and you would see men drinking from plastic cups, ordinary mugs, tea-can lids.

Someone would break wind loudly, followed by a disgusted voice saying, 'Ya dirty bastard. There's fuckin' men here eatin' ... why don't you go outside and fart?'

'It wasn't me,' someone would protest vehemently.

'It was you, ya dirty bastard.'

'Honest, it wasn't me.'

'It fuckin' was because you smell.' (loud laughter)

'He always smells,' someone added.

A little old Indian came to the door and complained about the noise. The man had a point, because it was around 3 a.m.

Someone told him to fuck off. 'Go on, Gandhi. Get fuckin' lost.'

Another voice protested, 'Let's keep the noise down, lads, or they will stop us using the mess room.'

A docker trying to get some sleep added his voice: 'The man's right. Keep the fuckin' noise down. I'm on in thirty minutes. Can't get no sleep here with you noisy bastards.'

Danny Kaye added to the confusion by saying, 'Right. Who wants to have a go at these questions?'

A sleepy voice piped up from the corner, 'Don't you fuckin' well start, Danny. It's bad enough in here without your fuckin' questions.'

Danny only laughed at this. He was never put off by hecklers. He only repeated what he had said. 'Who dares have a go at these questions? Who has the guts to try? Don't be scared. I'll make them easy for ya.'

The Angry Cat jumped in with 'Go ahead, Danny, ask me anything you like, especially movies or TV.'

Danny: 'Are you sure? Not biting off more than you can chew?'

Cat: 'Go ahead, Kaye. Get fuckin' on with it will ya?'

Man in a suitcase: 'Here ya, I've got one for ya, bet you don't get this.'

Cat: 'Wait your fuckin' turn.'

Danny: 'I'll make it easy for ya, OK?'

Cat: 'Don't do me any fuckin' favours. Do your worst.'

Danny: 'Right, I want you to tell me the name of the dog in the *Thin Man* series.'

Cat (snarling): 'What kind of a fuckin' question is that?'

Danny: 'A good one. What's up, too hard for ya?'

Fugitive: 'I know that dog's name …'

Danny: 'No one fuckin' asked you, don't worry, your turn will come and then we'll all have a good laugh.'

Unknown Soldier (raising his head from the table where he'd been trying to sleep): 'I think I know that one, Danny.'

Suitcase: 'Go back to sleep; no one fuckin' asked you.'

A tired voice from the other side of the mess room shouted, 'Why don't you all fuck off with your fuckin' stupid questions.'

Another sleeping man agreed. 'Yeah, go on, fuck off.'

Another butted in with 'Yeah, like the fucking Gladstone.' This always got a laugh, but Danny took it in his stride.

Danny: 'Come on Cat, answer the question. I thought you were the expert on TV. Ya don't fuckin' know, do ya?'

Cat: 'Can't just think of the name, but I did know, honest; it's slipped my mind at the moment.'

Danny: 'Why don't you stick to TV. Movies are too hard for you really.'

Cat: 'Fuck off. I've forgotten more than you will ever know.'

Danny: 'That will be the day. You couldn't spell your own fuckin' name until you met me.'

Man in a suitcase: 'Yeah, you know fuck all, Cat.'

Cat (getting all steamed): 'Go on, knowall, you fuckin' tell him. You don't know.'

Man in a suitcase: 'He didn't ask me the question.' And under his breath: 'I'm glad he didn't, just the same.'

Danny: 'OK, Cat. You don't know, do ya? Just say, "I don't know, O King".' He laughed like a maniac. 'The name of the dog was Asta. Now, don't forget. I'll ask you again later. You will have forgotten already.'

Cat: 'Alright, fuckin' knowall, heres one for you.'

Danny: 'Oh no, it's not your turn. You have to earn it. So I go again.'

Man in a suitcase: 'I hate him havin' another go.'

Fugitive: 'So do I.'

Danny: 'If that was too hard for ya, I'll make it a lot easier but really I shouldn't.'

This was how we used to spend our nightwork. Even when we left the mess room, the arguments would continue down the hatch. The time passed quicker anyway.

On the way back to the hatch, especially if it was forward of the bridge, it could be extremely dangerous. The deck leading up to your hatch could be like a minefield. Ringbolts welded to the deck – if you tripped over one of these, down you would go. There could be loose hatch-boards lying around, maybe the odd ventilator, even a rolled up tarpaulin. All these were obstacles that could cause minor bruises or even broken bones. There were deck lights of a sort, but these usually cast plenty of shadows everywhere. We usually went up forward on the opposite side to where the cargo was being brought in by crane or winches. The working side was extremely dangerous; you could be knocked over the side easily by a case on the hook going down the hatch. Even by the iron hook itself with a couple of rope slings hanging from it going back to the quay, or even a dirty oily wire under your chin or around your neck. I used to hate getting elected (by losing the toss) to go and make the tea aft in a dixie, and maybe half a dozen cups to wash out at the same time. That's if we had decided to have our tea break down the hatch. Then you had the return journey to make with the full can of boiling tea and the cups. Of course, if you got back to the hatch safely, you had to get the tea down to the lads below. You could either try your luck down the trunkway using one hand to grip the rungs in total darkness, or over the hatch coaming, which was practically suicidal! So you had to start looking around for some rope yarns to tie together to enable you to lower the lot down. By the time you found some, the tea would be cold or luke warm, and the lads would be screaming at your ineptitude. I have seen the rope yarns part half way down and the lot crash on the deck into a thousand pieces because, believe it or not, there were some men who could not make up a rope sling properly or tie their shoe lace, so how could you expect them to tie rope yarns together? The tears would be streaming down my face from laughing so much at their attempts, which wasn't fair really because some men just couldn't handle knots or hitches or shortening a rope or wire sling. I had had some experience before with being in the Merchant Navy for a few years. And then again some men just didn't want to know and somehow they got by. Apart from being embarrassed at not being able to shorten a sling or put a blackwall hitch on a hook, I thought it was your duty to learn and show a bit of interest. After all, it was part of your job.

The welt still went on during night work. Some men would work a night about, but I never fancied this at all. Two hours on and two off worked fine for me. Sometimes, depending on the type of cargo we were working, we would try and build a little hideaway among the cargo, just a small space where we could sit and drink our tea and have our butties and maybe get some sleep. One time, at a City boat, we were working cartons and carpets on nights, so we made a little room and fitted it out with carpets with easy access. We would even fit a carton or case at the entrance so no one would know it was there. Even the men working days would never find it. Of course, we were using valuable space that should have been used for cargo, but somehow we always managed to stow each and every item that was destined overseas. The only reason we did this was because sometimes, by the time you reached the mess room for your break, all the seats would be occupied by men working aft. If you were down No. 1 or No. 2, you had little chance of a speck in the mess room. Of course, in the winter, the mess room was a lot warmer than staying down below. If there had been access to a wall socket, we would definitely have brought a small electric fire to make us more comfortable. Funny thing, I remember the coldest part of the body while we were trying to get forty winks was the feet. It was great working nights in the summer but not so hot in the winter (pardon the pun), but you made your own fun to while away the hours. Some people called us the quiz kids, but it didn't bother us at all. Certainly, it never bothered me, because I have an inquisitive mind. The snarling that went on among us had to be seen and heard to be believed. But it was all in good humour; you simply had to be thick-skinned to take all the ribald humour:

'Saw your missus coming off a Greek ship this morning. She sure looked rough.'
'Oh, did she let on to you?'
'She never does … !'

Or

'How's your wife and my kids … ?'

Or

   'You told me your missus never gives you a blow job?'
   'That's correct.'
   'What made her change her mind?'

Or

   'Why didn't you tell me your wife snores?'

Of course, a lot of men couldn't accept this sort of humour, so one had to be careful not to upset anyone.

§

When the lads went to a ship, they all mustered in the shed and some jockeying went on. They sorted themselves out into gangs they knew they could rely on because, for the next week or so, they would be working the welt good style. Some men preferred the main hatch, No. 2 or perhaps No. 3. Number 2 was where the big stuff was stowed usually. As I said, No. 1 and No. 5 usually took the rubbish. But the biggest exception was that Clan ship that had whisky stowed in No. 5.

Sometimes you got split up from your friends and had to work with other men you didn't know. When I first started on the dock, before I started making friends with different people, I wasn't bothered which ship I was sent to or who I worked with. But after a while you get more choosy. You learn who to avoid. Men with a drink problem; men with glass backs who couldn't lift with you. Getting some men back from some dockside pub was a problem too. You could go on at 1 p.m. and expect to be finished at 3 and go home. But not always. The drinkers were disinclined to leave their beer and relieve their mates, so the unfortunate men were left on all afternoon. This was known as springboarding. Right off the top. Despicable, I always thought. You could possibly get your own back the following day, unless the other men were cleared out, in which case you couldn't do anything about it. You simply had to start again. But you knew who to avoid the next time. I don't know how such men could look in the mirror and not be ashamed. But there were such men who simply had no pride at all. I never did a job in because I just didn't happen to like it. No matter what we loaded, I stuck it out. That was the beauty of it; you took the rough with the smooth. I remember some characters going pale at the sight of a few hundred tons of bag-ash on the floor in the shed. They just couldn't face it. And I am talking about young men in their twenties and thirties, whereas older men would just get stuck in quietly and do it. I remember getting sent as a make-up to a Brocklebank ship as a replacement for a man who was absent. It was in the barge unloading bag-ash on boards to go into the ship. It was hard work. The men I joined told me the absentee had deliberately done the job in so he could go in the Pen with a chance of being hired for a billet ship that was due in at Rea's Wharf. These ships came in with heavy cargo such as steel billets or huge coils. As the crane did all the work, all you had to do was sling wires under or around the cargo and you were paid tonnage. And that could be considerable, far more than for breaking your back down below on another ship heading up drums of caustic. So, for a few hours' work, your wage packet was a lot thicker. And you still worked the welt. If you were in the Pen waiting to be hired and the boss, Joe Poole, walked out (this was the man from Rea's who hired for the billet ships), your legs could be broken in the stampede to get near him in the hope of being hired. I have seen him so frightened by the crowd, he beat a hasty retreat back to the office until everyone had calmed down. Never was a man so popular! I got lucky one afternoon when he hired me, but unfortunately that particular ship only paid buttons. Some men seemed to get these good-paying ships quite often, which made you think some faces were more popular than others.

The same man who did that job in came in drunk one night at 11 p.m. at another Clan ship; he was in our gang (unfortunately) and wanted to get his head down. We were loading two-hundredweight bags at the time and with four men away you need all the muscle you can get, so we threatened to get the timekeeper unless he got stuck in with us. I don't believe in carrying dead meat, especially characters like this man. Sometimes you got lumbered with them.

There was nothing you could do about it if they were sent from the Pen as make-up. Only once did I ever get sent to a ship as make-up to a gang that were not working the welt. Unbelievable. Joey B., the man who was acting stevedore, was getting carried away with himself. For some stupid reason, he wanted all hands on. So we had words. Besides, it was a cushy job, as they say; they were stowing large cases in the wings and a stacker was provided. So all you needed was two men really, but this prick wanted to be awkward. One man could have done the job, placing battens so the driver could get his forks out from under. But on this particular easy job, we always let the driver go for his ale if he so desired, and one of us would drive the stacker. That job didn't finish too soon for me.

§

For most of my time on the docks I never knew the real names of many dockers. Of course, you might know their Christian names but never their surnames. You might know some but not all. For example, I never knew Harry Worth's or Harry the Birdman ... or Nose and Glasses. It was always a first name or nickname. You could be working with the likes of the Wolfman, TV Times, the Werewolf, Chocolate Mouse, the Angry Cat, Joe 90, the Saint, Beast with Five Fingers, the Snarling Swede, Machine Gun, Tween deck Jimmy, Blackpan Alf, Silver Bullet, the Quiet Man. I don't think there is an industry anywhere in the world that contains so many marvellous and sometimes ingenious nicknames. And each one was given with imagination. 'The Beast with Five Fingers'? Well, the story is that he was observed masturbating down the hatch. He always denied this and protested he was only urinating in a corner! 'Hercules' – a name to conjure with. But in this case it was a misnomer because strongman he was not. Harry the Birdman fancied himself as an amateur ornithologist. Quiet man and very pleasant to work with. The man with no arms – you never saw his arms move when he was walking. Friday Frank – always took that afternoon off whether he was on or off. Just too bad if you were in the opposite welt to him. The Ugly Guardsman, Dr Beaker, Lino, Me and Her, Sharkhead, Lardhead, Doubleheaded Docker, the Bandy Hen, the Duck, Quasimodo, Porthole Pet, the Singing Docker. These are just a few of the colourful names given to men I have worked alongside. There are many more I shall be mentioning later. Each one was a character of some sort whether outgoing or introverted; that's what made the docks so interesting and stimulating. There was always something happening. There might be a whisper someone had got to the whisky down the hatch at another ship, or the cigarettes ... a watchman had been found dead sitting in a corner ... so and so had been caught going out the gate with his pockets full of toothpaste tubes ... police activity at a Harrison ship that was loading whisky – some of the lads were drunk and causing trouble and objecting to the police coming down the hatch to search them ... a girl at a certain ship was charging a pound a man for a short time – she was in a crew members cabin aft and anybody was welcome. No thanks!

§

I won't bore the reader with uninteresting statistics about the volume of work on the docks, except that Liverpool and Birkenhead were extremely busy during the Fifties and Sixties, even Ellesmere port and Manchester. I can remember when there would be well over a dozen ships at anchor in the Mersey, even ships at the Bar waiting to come in to berth when one became vacant. I suppose it was sometimes a big headache for the river pilots dodging all that shipping. Almost forgot the once-busy little dock of Garston with its grimy colliers and timber boats. The river was extremely busy in those days with ships of all shapes and sizes coming and going; the ferry boats had to do a fair bit of dodging during their numerous crossings from Liverpool to Wallasey and Birkenhead. Now they could do it blindfolded. Back in 1960, there were 16,000 dockers on Merseyside and well over a hundred ships working full time. Sometimes surplus dockers from Manchester would come up to help man the ships in Liverpool and Birkenhead. Ellesmere Port docks, situated a few miles down the Manchester ship canal, was once a busy place; they handled a variety of cargo too. I didn't mind discharging timber and pulp but hated the sulphur some ships brought – your eyes would be streaming continuously despite a mask and special goggles. But most of the pulp was discharged a few hundred yards away at Bowaters wharf. I remember ships passing up and down the MSC fairly frequently; with a tug fore and aft, the large vessels would make their way down to Manchester. I spent about six months working on Ellesmere Port docks, and they did not work the welt at all. But I spent most of my working time at Birkenhead, and most of that down below in the hold. I loved every minute of it and was never bored. It was only later during my last four years on the docks that I finished up on the quay in the capacity they called 'stowing back'; in fact, we were called 'stowbacks'. All it meant really was that we worked with a quay foreman who told us where to lay the cargo down on the quay that was brought in by road or rail transport, either in the sheds or outside in the avenues near the ship. This gave me and a friend who I shall refer to as J.D. a golden opportunity to help ourselves to what we could take away and sell, and there was a market for most articles we handled. But it soon became apparent to the authorities and the dock police that when we were around a lot of stuff went missing. But we were quite aware of the situation.

It did not deter us. It became a sort of game keeping one (or two) steps ahead of the police. Where we used to walk off a ship with loot stashed on our person playing Russian roulette with a few items, we now used commercial vehicles, vans or twenty- to forty-foot trailers. For instance, if we had twenty tons of sheet steel, angle iron, compressors, or even tractors, we would ring our contact. He might have a tractor unit but no trailer. No problem. There were always plenty around the dock estate. We would simply back the unit up and couple the trailer up to the lights and brake pipes, release the brake and off we would go.

We would then load a trailer with the goods and if necessary tie and chock the lot. Then we would get out of the way until the unit arrived from out of town. While we were waiting, we would make sure that we hadn't been tumbled by anyone. A special watch would be kept on the dock police vans, which used to roam all over the place. We knew the movements of these vehicles and the drivers, but we never took anything for granted. Sometimes, the trailer we 'borrowed' we just left after we had finished with it, or now and again we would bring it back to the dock estate and just leave it anywhere.

We never took unnecessary chances. Everything was thought out and calculated. But anything could happen and did. For example, we had just loaded two large compressors onto a trailer in the Golden Mile area (near Duke Street bridge, Wallasey); we had even chocked the wheels and roped it. The trailer was outside the shed ready and we were just about to move it when a little old watchman came out of the shed to fill his kettle with water at a tap on the wall. He was very sharp despite his advanced years and tumbled right away what was going on. That little old man's tea break cost us a lot of money.

He scuttled back inside the shed to get to a phone. I told our driver to get going immediately and drive a few hundred yards away from the dock estate out of sight and then abandon the vehicle. If all went well and the police didn't notice it, we would still be in business. I knew the driver would have plenty of time to do this, but for some reason, after he had driven away, he stayed in his cab. He was arrested and charged. We saw the whole thing from a safe distance but could do nothing about it. If he had listened and done as he was told he would have been in the clear.

We expected the worst because we didn't know this particular driver well enough. He might well implicate us, so we were prepared for a visit. Incredibly, after a week in Risley remand centre, he went up before the Magistrates and they believed his story: he had been approached by two men and asked to move a large vehicle from the dock estate and park it nearby ready for another driver to take it away. Being out of work, he had jumped at the chance to earn some money. He had no idea the compressors had been stolen, and had he known, he would never have got involved. The Magistrates warned him to be more careful in future who he worked for. They fined him £50 and let him go. Naturally, J.D. and I were very relieved. For a while, our jobs and freedom hung in the balance. We paid his fine. So we lived to fight another day.

§

J.D. and I managed to take away well over sixty tons of pure copper. All this within the space of less than a year. We used various forms of transport. We knew a lot of other men who managed to get some copper too, but always had to burn the outer cover off before they could sell it. They would have to take it somewhere private and build a fire to do so. But we always seemed to be dead lucky with ours. It was always pure with no outer cover. And we always got the huge wooden reels. In the Sixties, around about '66 or '67, it used to fetch about sixteen pounds a hundredweight. At first, I used to take it out in the boot of my mini, but you are hampered by lack of space. So we started using vans, and eventually larger vehicles. Cupronickel sold well, as did bronze, lead, steel. It was all the same to us. If we could sell it, we would take it. As they say, if there were no receivers, there would be no stealers. Naturally, we never got the full price for all this stuff. There was definitely no honour among the villains we did business with. What J.D. and I didn't realise was that these people had been stealing all their lives. They were conmen. They must have thought it was Christmas every time we got them stuff. But I will admit a few times I had toyed with the idea of stockpiling the stuff somewhere safe, under lock and key. And then acting like a salesman, try and get the best prices. I had a few contacts here and there.

But it never came off because it would have been too dangerous. As it turned out, it couldn't have been any worse. I know for a fact that most of the people we dealt with were not capable of handling what we could have given them. It was too big for them. It would have been a very different story if we had met just one man who could have. We could have taken brand-new export cars any time; they were offloaded from the transporters and left on the quay in the avenue. We used to take parts we needed from different export models, usually the wipers, batteries, spare wheels, parts from the engine, plus the tool kits. They were all saleable. I remember stripping a brand-new mini for myself. And this took place down below in the hold.

When I had got enough parts, I sent it ashore on a board. But really this was doing it the hard way. What I should have done was drive the car from the docks.

§

We were working days on a Clan boat at Lewis's Quay and were leaving the ship about 4.50 p.m. to go home. Walking down the deck from No. 1

hatch we saw Jason B. on the quay sprawled out across some pallet boards. He was on his back out to the world. We already knew the lads had got the whisky going down the after hatch and had been having a ball. When we reached the quay where he was lying, we saw he was in a bad way. I cleaned the vomit from his face with my handkerchief and then I backed my car up to the shed door. We then tried to lift him but found we couldn't. It was also impossible to get him into the car because of his size. I think he was about sixteen stone, but he sure was heavier with all that whisky inside him. I felt his pulse because he was hardly breathing but I couldn't feel anything, so we decided to call an ambulance just to be on the safe side. After the ambulance had taken him away, I decided to call at his house on my way home and tell his wife he would be a little late getting home. I explained what had happened and told her not to worry. She took it quite calmly, saying, 'He's getting off them fuckin' docks. They're doin' him no good at all.'

We found out later that they had to put a straitjacket on Jason before they could pump out the whisky in his body. It was funny at the time, but it could have been fatal for him. What I did not understand was why he was left lying there in the first place. There is usually someone who is not so far gone in the gang who could have looked after him. I have seen men so drunk they could not climb the ladder out of the hatch so have to be taken out in a tub by crane. Men have fallen off the quay and would have gone into the water if not for the rope nets that were strung out to catch falling cargo during loading. It was funny to see them trying to get out but finding it impossible.

§

Bobby W. pedalled out of the dock gate with a lavatory pan tied to his bike. And got away with it. I will ignore the obvious pun about his success.

§

The Silver Bullet was ordered to see the Manager in the Admin Building at Vittoria Dock because of something he had done. He was working at the North Quay on a City boat on the Golden Mile. He decided to take a leisurely stroll down the quay and be in plenty of time for the confrontation with the Manager. The Bullet took his time. It was just after 1 p.m. and the meeting was at 1.30.

Meanwhile, in the Manager's office, the Manager kept looking at his watch. The shop-steward said not to worry, the Bullet would definitely turn up. Two hours passed and the Manager was getting agitated. 'I can't wait all day. I have other work to do.' The steward was starting to become impatient too. Another half an hour elapsed and the Bullet turned up.

'What happened?' asked the steward.

Duke Street bridge had been up in the air for about nine months due to repair work that was being carried out. Despite the fact that no ships were coming through, it did not dawn on the Bullet that the bridge was not coming down. After standing there for over two hours, someone told him. It seemed that everyone else knew the bridge was off except him. The look on the Manager's face was one of pure incredulity.

§

B.L., a holdsman, was coming off the nights at the Mortar Mill berth. Just as he and a number of other men reached the first bridge, it swung off to allow a ship through. It was still in the Alfred basin and would be quite a while. But B.L. was desperate to go to a toilet for a bodily function and couldn't wait. He lived near the dock and intending to make for home. The dockside toilets at that time were rather primitive. So he dived into the dock and swam across and hauled himself out the other side. He walked the rest of the way soaking wet.

§

Every so often a van would arrive on the quay at the various sheds. It was called the Boot Van. You could enter the back of the van and take your pick of dozens of different styles of protective boots or shoes. Steel toecaps also if you wanted. You either paid the man there and then or paid on the drip (five shillings a week). This was deducted from your wages until they were paid for. I have watched men go in and buy boots and then walk out and sell them for less money just to buy booze. But then some men would sell their soul to the devil himself.

A docker who shall be nameless once 'found' a paybook and with it purchased six pairs of boots on credit from the boot van. He was found out and thumped for it. There was even talk of a strike over the incident.

§

A chap called Rachman (after the notorious landlord) was up a ladder down below trying to fix a block to the deck-head to be used for heaving in. He was smoking at the same time. Just for a laugh one of the lads called out, 'Jesus, he's young for a sergeant, isn't he?' Rachman nearly had a coronary and dropped the block right away, narrowly missing another man's head. Smoking was strictly forbidden on the quay or down the hatch.

§

Flatfoot Joney Holdsman was very bad on his plates. I mean no disrespect to anyone with less than perfect health but this man suffered. One day he had an appointment with a chiropodist and was seen making his way down the dock road. A friend asked him where he was going.

'On me way to the chiropodist,' Joney replied.

'You should get at least ten nights out of her,' his friend said.

§

On a Blue Star ship that was discharging meat, slings were not too full coming ashore. Joe the Blow (ship's boss) happened to notice one such sling coming out of the hatch and shouted down to the holdsmen, 'Try and get some more on those boards will ya. The seagulls got the last lot.'

The Tipster: 'I'll bet this ship will be a week of five o'clocks.'

Dr Barnard: 'No early dart here; have a heart boss …'

§

Creeping Paralysis was a checker whose movements made a sloth look very fast. Billy B. was known as the Clan Ghost. He used to put a nylon stocking over his face and frighten the unwary, especially the ladies who used to visit the ships to give solace to many a lonely seaman.

§

When you went to a ship, you were supposed to keep to your own hatch. It was the luck of the draw what cargo you were to handle. You could be down No. 5 loading all sorts of drums, bags, cartons. Most times there wasn't anything worth stealing down No. 1 and No. 5 hatches, but every now and then you could find something like aftershave, soap or toothpaste, even razor blades. We have even stowed this sort of stuff in the fo'castle head. No. 1 and No. 5 were called the shit hatches because of the type of cargo that was stowed in those particular hatches. But not always. One notable exception was a certain Clan ship I worked on that had whisky stowed in a cage at the after-end. More about that later. If you were working in a hatch that had something for the bag then your luck was in (if you were a bagman). You could have mates working down another hatch who might have the whisky going, but it was bad policy to trespass into another hatch. It went on though. You were expected to keep away, but there were always the greedy people who disregarded this rule and caused untold trouble by doing so. Too many men down a hatch attracted attention from the watchmen and ship's officers. Certain men who had a drink problem (and there were quite a few), once they smelled whisky, would hang around on the bum until someone gave them a bottle, and they would then disappear for a while. If you didn't give them a bottle, you were the biggest bastard on the docks. But these particular men didn't care as long as they got a drink. When you had the whisky going, you tried to keep it quiet for as long as you could, because once other people got wind of it, they would come around like bees around honey. You suddenly had friends you never knew before. Plus there was the danger of the security people and customs getting wind of it. You could go so long before it all blew up and then you had to be very careful. Also dangerous was your own mates drinking on the job down below. Naturally, the more they drank the slower the job progressed. Then the boss would want to know what was going on.

The dock police would be hovering around the quay just waiting to pounce. Once you were full of whisky you took chances, the police became invisible. Too late once you were on the quay making your way to the gate with a couple of bottles in your belt. Then the pull and search and there goes your job. I saw it happen many times. A lot of men needed a few drinks to give them a little courage. Stupid. If you are going to carry, stay sober, because you need all your wits about you. The drink lost a lot of men a good job. It also stopped me and a few friends from making some money because we did not touch the stuff whilst carrying from the ship and off the dock estate. I used to plead with them not to drink until we had taken our stuff from the ship, but it was a waste of time asking. Then we had to contend with the usual banter about being greedy and tight. Not so. We didn't care how much they drank as long as it didn't interfere with our business.

On one occasion, J.J. was at the Bidston Dock carrying two bottles of whisky along the quay. Out steps the Farmer's Boy (dock police). J.J. promptly took the bottles from under his clothing and walked to the edge of the quay and smashed the bottles together and the broken glass fell into the water. He turned and grinned at the policeman. Case dismissed for lack of evidence ...

I have another example of this. A chap was going out the gate in Liverpool with a few bottles of whisky and was stopped by the police. He refused to be searched, so they locked him up. The man had had a few drinks and it looked like the end for him. But some colleagues helped him out when he passed the bottles out to them from a small window. No evidence. So he lived to fight another day.

Another time, we were working down below on a Japanese ship at the East Quay, a Henderson berth. Myself, Harry the Birdman, Big Bobby Weir and Man with No Arms. I can't remember the other four men. We filled the lower hold with general cargo and put the hatch-boards on. We were now in the tween deck level and the locker was about to be filled with whisky, which was good news, if we could get at it. But the bad news was one of the Japanese crew was going to watch us. But, as they say, where there is a will ... Sooner or later our luck would change, and it did. The poor man couldn't watch the man inside the locker and the men landing the sling. We managed to get a dozen bottles of Cutty Sark out of one of the cardboard cases and hid them out of sight of the watchman.

The ship was on the finish, so they were in a hurry to get the whisky stowed so they could put a padlock on it. We managed to get some Ballantine's out too and the lads were having a gargle. With about five slings to go, the job started to slow down. Bobby was starting to sing, the Birdman's eyes were glowing like coals and he was muttering away, no one could understand a word he was saying. The watchman was getting very uptight about the way things were going; he was wondering why Harry kept falling down and staggering carrying cases into the locker. If he couldn't see anyone drinking, he must have smelled it. He would check the inside of the locker, but I had hidden bottles on the shelf just inside the door.

I was trying to work out how I could get some bottles out and up the ladder without dropping any. Then the ship's boss started shouting down for us to hurry up. Big Bobby just snarled up at him, 'Why don't you just fuck off.' More threats from the boss. He could see three men staggering. Then the watchman started to argue with us, telling us to hurry, in Japanese, of course. Bobby turned on him: 'Fuck off, prick. Don't you start. Remember Pearl Harbor. Slimy bastards ...' I couldn't stop laughing at that. The man was too young to remember. We managed to get the last board finished and made our way to the ladder to get out of the hatch. A row of Japanese faces were looking down at us. Some were smiling; the officers were not. The ship's boss was happy now. I had managed to stash three bottles on me and waited for Bobby to try and get up on deck. He climbed a couple of rungs and then came back down again; one of his bottles fell out and smashed on the deck causing uproar. He just grinned and managed to climb onto the main deck, followed by Harry, who fell over. The hatch boss warned us that Lloydy and the Farmer's Boy were in the shed. I took no chances and smashed my bottles on the side of the quay. I had a Lambretta scooter at that time, but I had to leave it because I had had a couple of mouthfuls. I don't usually drink, but I got into the party spirit. As far as I know, nobody got pulled by the police. I do remember going home by bus and sleeping in the backyard for a few hours. Disgraceful I must admit. It was the first and last time. I was really in the dog house and deservedly so.

The following is a sample of dialogue down a hatch when the whisky was going:

'Lloydy and the Farmer are on the quay,' someone remarked.

'Fuck 'em, pair of bastards.'

'I wouldn't take those bottles. Leave 'em. Just askin' for trouble.'

'No fuckin' chance. I'm takin' them ashore.'

'You're gonna walk right into them,' said another voice.

'The watchman is gonna have a heart attack if you take them bottles. He's watchin' you. Probably lose his fuckin' job over this.'

'Why don't you leave the bottles somewhere and get them tomorrow when the coast is clear?'

'What are you? Some kind of fuckin' coast guard? Fuck 'em, I'm takin' them now.'

'Where's Billy?'

'He's out of the game.' (Billy was throwing up in a corner.)

'What's the hold up?' shouted a voice from the deck. It was the Manager.

'Jesus Christ,' said Humpty Dumpty, 'it's the fuckin' manager. Three men tryin' to keep this job goin'. Get Billy, quick.'

Billy staggered to his feet; his eyes were glazed and he swayed, almost falling. 'What's goin' on?' he slurred.

'Get over here, Billy, and get on this board and pass some cases in. The fuckin' Manager's over the hatch.'

'Come over,' Billy shouted to the deckhand. He was unaware there was already a board full of whisky outside the cage entrance. The deckhand just smiled down at Billy. The Manager wasn't smiling. He shouted down again.

'What the fuck does he want?' asked Billy, with a silly grin on his face.

'The job isn't goin' fast enough,' replied Humpty. 'Come on, get hold of some of these cases or we are all gonna get cleared out. Four men away you know …'

Billy staggered over to the ladder and started looking for the bottom rung but couldn't find it. He was on the point of collapse.

'Get over here, ya soft prick. Where d'ya think your goin?' Humpty was full of whisky himself but was endeavouring to carry some cases into the cage. Billy staggered over to the board, grabbed a case of whisky and tried to carry it into the cage but tripped and fell. The old watchman looked very worried and got out of the way. Billy cursed, staggered to his feet and said, 'Ah, fuck it. I've had enough I'm goin …' and started for the ladder again.

He managed to climb three rungs and then fell to the deck and lay in a crumpled heap at the foot of the ladder. Humpty saw what happened and went over to see if Billy was hurt. He wasn't hurt at all; he was just fast asleep and out of the game altogether. Just then, the other four men came back and started climbing down the ladder. They each stepped over Billy.

'What happened to him?' asked the Mangy Cat.

'It's fuckin' obvious,' snarled Action Man. 'Can't you see he's out the game? Can't leave him there. Let's carry him into the wing and then we'll send him out in a tub later if he's still out.'

Billy was picked up and taken to a safe place and left to sleep it off.

'Come on, let's get stuck in,' said Action Man. 'The Manager's still over the hatch. That bastard will clear us all out no bother.'

The above scene I witnessed many times. Some were much worse but they were always hilarious. A lot of men did not take anything off a ship, but if they liked a drink they would attack the whisky and drink it like it was the elixir of life itself, and especially if it was free. Straight from the bottle or from plastic cups if they were available. These men wouldn't dream of taking any bottles from the ship, but if it was obtainable down below, it was open season.

§

Big A. got the whisky going at the Mortar Mill quay. He sold some to the crew, which was often done. No one was going to look a gift horse in the mouth. One of the Indians on the ship was unfortunately caught by the police. He immediately put the finger on Big A. and blamed him. Big A. thought quickly and adopted a disguise so the Indian could not point him out to the police. Glasses, hat, different coat and adopted a walk like Groucho Marx. The Indian was baffled.

§

Birkenhead docks was a loading port. Sometimes we would get the odd ship in to discharge some cargo, maybe a few hundred tons. I never saw a ship come in fully loaded and be discharged while I was there. There is a lot of skill in loading a ship. Every item is well planned before the ship even gets in to be loaded. Each of the five hatches has its own particular cargo and port of destination. The cargo had to be loaded in order of the ship's ports of call. For example, if Beira or Dar es Salaam were last out, it would be loaded first. And the cargo had to be loaded in such a way according to weight and distribution to keep the ship on an even keel. Nothing must be allowed to come adrift and start rolling or sliding about to upset the equilibrium. Once this particular port was finished, the cargo was separated by using long strips of wood called slabs. These are laid down across these cases and then the other port is placed on top; to avoid any confusion, most of the cases are marked with the port or destination painted on with a light-blue water paint. But mistakes do happen and the wrong cargo is sent in, but in most cases it is discovered and then has to be dug out.

First in the hold was the heavy stuff. This could be anything from sheet steel to drums of caustic to large cases containing machinery or such. The heavy wooden cases were stoutly made to withstand some weight. The wood was thick and had thick battens around it; sometimes it was banded with steel bands. Most times when I was below, the first things sent in were the large case cars, huge wooden cases. These were landed in the middle of the hold and then would have to be heaved into the wings (ship's sides). This could be twenty or thirty feet, so wires and pulley blocks would have to be used. This was a fairly uncomplicated job; once the blocks on the deck-head were placed in a good position, all that was required was the winch heaving the piece into position. The art was positioning the appropriate blocks in the best position. You could floor out (completely cover the deck of a hatch) with drums of caustic and, when this is completed, cover the lot with wooden slabs and start again. These drums came in the hatch on chains, six at a time sometimes. You had to roll them into the wings and then head them up. It took two men lifting together to lift one up, but it was possible to lift one yourself (if you were strong enough). Sometimes the drums would come in eight at a time; we would throw the chains off and start rolling them in quickly. If we were quick enough, we would have a breather before the next lot came in. But we had to keep the job going, because the other four men were away. But sometimes a drum would fall down a hole somewhere and get wedged. If we couldn't man-handle it out, we would have to get the fall to help us drag it out. Many a grazed shin has befallen me during this particular job. Rolling the drums in over the slabs wasn't too bad, but if you caught the end of a slab, it could fly up and smack you in the face or sometimes even between your legs, so you had to be very careful.

The only problem with placing slabs down over the cargo was the fact that it could be very dangerous. You could easily scrape your shins or break a leg if you missed your footing as you worked over it or were carrying cases. A slab could easily be dislodged and down you would go. Happened to me many times but the most that happened to me was scraped shins or slightly damaged ankles. But I have fallen full length. As you are falling, you just hope your face doesn't hit anything on the way down. It was just one of the hazards of the job. Most of the lads wore steel toecaps in their boots because some of those little cases (we called them nuggets) could be a couple of hundredweight, and if one happened to turn over onto your toes, it could break one quite easily. You could be heaving a case over with your hook and suddenly it became detached and away you would go.

I had a very nasty experience once down the hatch of a Brocklebank ship. I was trying to turn a case over with my hook and suddenly I was flying through the air. I fell about six feet into the lower ground, which was full of cases, but luckily I hit none of them. I cursed for a while and told my mates I was having no more of it and would pack the job in soon. But I didn't. You learn to do things the easy way instead of going at it like a crazy man. Never take chances and always make certain of your footing. It was like a minefield below sometimes. It was fine when you were just starting off on the 'skin' – this is what we called the floor or the deck of the hatch. Everything was smooth, but as you progressed upwards so it got more hazardous and more care had to be taken. Heavy drums were especially awkward when you were trying to head them up (put them right way up) onto a wooden deck consisting of laid slabs. If a drum slipped, it would smash the slabs quite easily and a piece could hit you under the chin, so you had to be very careful how you worked on such ground.

The cargo came in all shapes and sizes and of course different weights. Sometimes you were loading a particular cargo of drums or cases that were all the same size, which made things a lot easier and quicker. We were made up to get cases all the same size and a stacker truck down below. This meant a good time for all. Only two men were normally required to assist the driver by placing battens to enable his forks to clear. So there would be only two men on instead of eight. And even then one of the two men on would let the driver go for his beer (if he was so inclined) and most were. Most of the lads could drive a stacker, although they never held a full licence, but down below they were safe enough. But some of them still had to be watched, and you never turned your back on them. But suddenly the good time would be over and that particular cargo would finish; the hatch boss would usually tell you what was happening, and you would have time to get the welt back to normal. That stacker certainly saved a lot of hard work.

Of all the drums we loaded at the docks the most dreaded were the big drums of Octel, from Ellesmere Port. They came down by road and parked up on the quay alongside the ship and were winched aboard and landed on the main deck on their rolling way. Each drum weighed seven hundredweight, possibly nine – it varied. It took three men using a short rope to lift one up on its end. Then it had to be positioned correctly, and this was the hardest part of the job. There was usually a representative from Octel watching that you did so. After all these drums were stowed on the main deck on slabs, they were secured with wire and tightened using bottle screws. The only time I ever saw them stowed down below was at a Blue Funnel ship. I remember in the tween decks trying to head them up using the same method and it was murder. We had floored out and put slabs down and were going on top. The space was very restricted and heads were getting cracked on the overhead beams (at that time no safety helmets were worn). We never got any thanks for working in such conditions, and it was a struggle sometimes.

I might add that the drums of caustic we handled many times weighed seven hundredweight and all had to be headed up before someone realised it wouldn't do any harm to leave them on their rolling way. A lot of our handball jobs called for red faces and wet shirts and strained vertebrae. It was essential to have a partner who pulled his weight in heading up all those heavy drums, otherwise you could end up in traction. My partner at that Blue Funnel ship that took a full hatch of Octel was Andy the Liar, and I couldn't have asked for a better man. Definitely the worst job I ever had on the docks, but you took the rough with the smooth of course.

You could go into the Pen and get one of the cushiest jobs, like being sent to one of the big cranes, such as the *Atlas* or the *Mammoth*. All you had to do was sling the thick wires under the huge cases or maybe a 50-ton compressor or locomotive and stand well clear. The hardest part of this job was climbing up a ladder up the ship's side. The crane would be alongside the quay and would pick up all the cargo destined for a particular ship's hatch. This was a slow job because all the pieces were very big and extremely heavy. Once you had all these stowed on the deck, you cast off and made your way to the ship. Then you would secure the crane alongside the ship and start unloading. Some of the lifts were awesome to look at, especially the locos or huge transformers. The *Mammoth* could lift just over 200 tons even though she was well over sixty years old. Built in Holland in 1920. She must have seen plenty of action during the Second World War. I was a child playing in the street a few hundred yards away when she was loading tanks, bulldozers, guns and ammunition aboard the many American Liberty ships that thronged the many quays and wharves at that time. I remember sneaking aboard a small coastal vessel at Rea's Wharf and looking with fascination at the boxes of expended bullet cases before I was escorted from the ship and told to keep off. Little did I know, much later I would go to sea for a short while and then finish up on the docks! Working on the big cranes meant more money for less work, as you were paid tonnage. Once we had finished our work on the crane, you reported back to the Pen if it wasn't too late. If you finished early enough, you could possibly be sent as a make-up, or if there were enough men, you could be sent out on nights.

Another unwelcome job we had to do sometimes was loading dusty hessian bags. There would be a paper bag inside, but they were always dirty with clouds of dust floating around them. Or paper bags marked Lembuks, another filthy dusty job. This was before we were issued with facemasks and gloves. It got that bad even with these precautions that we had to get away from the dust cloud and get on the main deck to get some fresh air before tackling the job again. But the most trying job was when we were in the deep tanks loading these bags and similar. The most common was bag-ash. There would be four men in a deep tank and the deckhand would come over and try and get the board with about twenty-four to thirty bags on it into the tank. Of course, the derrick would be plumbed over the entrance but the load would be swinging about all over the place. He would lower sometimes at the wrong time and the board would tip, spilling the load on top of us. There was nowhere to run, so we would be coughing and spluttering and trying to get up the ladder to take a breather. Sometimes we did not know exactly what commodity was in the bags. A lot of them were unmarked, so for all we knew they could have been toxic. But most of the bags we handled were clearly marked and had instructions on what to do if your skin or eyes came into contact with it. If we did find out that certain bags were toxic although unmarked, we would ask for a few shillings more as danger money. But most times the management didn't want to know, so we ended up in dispute and walked off the ship. How often have you heard the expression 'lazy dockers'? Ignorant people were quick to criticise us, but they would never know the reason why there were so many disputes. If they had only known the circumstances surrounding some strikes we had, they might have kept their opinions to themselves.

Those so-called knockers would have been the first to scream at some of the things that happened to some of the lads working on certain foreign ships that didn't believe in maintenance of their vessels. Like the unfortunate docker working on the main deck of a Greek tramp. He was helping to stow ordinary-looking drums when one sprang a leak and some liquid splashed onto his private parts. The stuff actually burnt through his clothes, and when the lads tried to turn on the water from a deck pipe, it was seized solid. In the meantime, the man with the burning parts is suffering agonies of mind thinking the worst. But luckily he wasn't seriously injured. Other unfortunate men have been injured down below and had to suffer the indignity of being taken out in a dirty wooden tub, probably full of broken earthenware pipes and filthy straw. The men in the street didn't have a clue what went on on the docks, or some women for that matter, but they were quick to call them if they heard they were on strike. I will admit some strikes were bloody stupid and a complete waste of time. Some men only put their hands up to strike so they could spend the time in some boozer. I would like to mention the footballers here. Some dockers got carried away with their weekend run around the field. So much so it affected their work down below. They would act like prima donnas. Rolling drums terrified them, or turning a case over it would be, 'For Christ's sake, watch my feet,' or, 'Watch my legs will ya …' Anyone would think we had Pelé or Eusébio down the hatch. They were more concerned with their physical well-being than helping you with a heavy case that had to be hooked into the wings. Any minute you would expect one of them to offer his autograph. The only footballer down below who would get stuck in regardless was a Liverpool chap called 'The Mighty Quinn'; he was great company to work with. The others were a pain in the neck.

§

A docker asked Big Nose for permission to go to a cremation at Landican, promising to get back as soon as possible.

'No problem son,' said Big Nose (ship's boss), take your time, but I would ring them up if I was you, and ask them to keep him on a low light until you get there …'

§

Someone asked Addo where he'd been for dinner. 'Oh, I was in the menagerie,' explaining he had been in the company of Crazy Horse, Morris the Mouse, Old Grey Mare and the Rocking Horse.

§

Myself, Man in a Suitcase and the Leper were making our way across Vittoria bridge on our way to the Sweat Box, a local dockside café just outside the gate. We bumped into Andy the Liar making his way back to the ship.

Andy: 'Just took £80 off the bookie again!'

Leper: 'That's good news, Andy. So show us the money then.'

Andy: 'He didn't have enough cash to pay me, so I have to go back later.'

Leper: 'You're a fuckin' liar, Andy. How is it we never see any of this money you keep takin' off the bookie?'

Andy (with a pained look on his face): 'Honest. He just didn't have enough cash to pay me.'

Leper: 'Well, at least show us the ticket, or a receipt, and then maybe we'll believe you.'

I felt sorry for the man, but he did tell terrible lies. He had no need to because he was a nice guy and a very hard worker. I always liked his company when he was in the gang.

§

When you enter any hatch to start work the first and most important thing you do is check to make certain that there are safety lines in place, especially the tween decks. These are usually rope or wire about waist high surrounding the open hatch. I never saw one that would have stopped a man falling down below. Of course, they were there as a warning too. They were usually found hanging slack, and most times we had to tighten them up as best we could. Really, there should have been nets over waist high to be effective. This was the crew's job, but as they say, if you want a proper job doing, do it yourself. Same with the beams – we used to do these as well before we would call the crew out. As I've said, it was murder sometimes trying to dislodge one that was jammed good and proper. We used to do stupid things like walking across a beam to the other side of the hatch with a drop of twenty or thirty feet below. Sheer bravado on anyone's part, but I have done it myself. It was a long way down and a steel deck to fall on. Of course, men have fallen down hatches but not because of this. Accidents did happen, but sometimes for the wrong reason. For example, one man decided to have a go at the whisky one night when the hatch was closed. Everything is pitch black down there with no lights on at all. He missed his footing and fell, getting badly hurt in the process. His friends got him ashore somehow and left him on the quay to make it look like the accident had happened there, and he also was paid a substantial amount in damages.

§

Mars Bar had the misfortune to fall down a hatch and luckily escaped unhurt. A docker was overheard saying, 'He was fuckin' lucky he fell on his head.' Others weren't so lucky. A docker went missing for four days. He was eventually found at the bottom of the dock. His bike was found nearby. George S. was accidentally knocked from the main deck onto the quay. He suffered a broken back and spent the next two years in traction.

§

The Penguin was in Southport with some other dockers on a day out. He decided to ring home and find out if everything was all right. But he didn't use the dialling code for his area and found himself talking to a complete stranger. 'What the fuckin' hell are you doing in my house?' he screamed down the phone. He thought he was being burgled. But all that had happened was he had phoned someone in their own home.

§

Jack R. Holdsman was working on a skin boat (Elders & Fyffes) at Garston, where spiders are not uncommon among the bananas. He was complaining most of the time about spiders and snakes all over the place but everyone knew it was really the DTs he was suffering from.

§

J.D. and I found some tea chests in the shed one day full of brass ornaments. We knew they were very saleable, so we decided to take the lot. So we hired a skip and had it places on the quay against the side of the shed. Our mistake was it was in full view of the ship but just aft of the stern. It was a Greek tramp and we underestimated the intelligence of her crew. So we proceeded to fill the skip up with these rather heavy tea chests using a stacker-truck.

When this was done, we threw bits of wood and some rubbish on top to disguise it. We patted ourselves on the back on a job well done and waited for the unit to come and collect the skip. We had been standing on the quay for a few minutes talking when we saw one of the crew pointing in our direction. He was accompanied by a ship's officer and he was going on good style in Greek, but we got the message and made ourselves scarce. Sure enough, the Law arrived a few minutes later, but as we were not around, no one could put the finger on us. So that was one we lost.

§

Funny thing happened at a Safmarine ship one time. A.M. was a deckhand and had to reposition a derrick, so he threw some turns off a cleat on the bulwarks. What he didn't know was that two Cape crewmen were over the side working on a stage painting and they both fell into the water. To add insult to injury, they were splashed with paint. Luckily, it was summertime, so the water wasn't so cold.

§

Steve R. (hatch boss) was working on a Harrison ship. He was knocked down by a sling and had a leg broken. He was lying on the deck in some pain when the ship's boss came along.

'What the hell have you done?' he asked Steve.

'Eighty ton before dinner,' Steve replied, grimacing.

§

There was a certain policeman who worked on the docks who was a pure bastard. Mitchell. He would pull anyone up and search them. He even stopped the nurses who worked in the first-aid department. Hoppy S. was a deckhand who decided to teach this man a lesson. Hoppy used to own an old gas mask case which he used to put horse droppings in. This was during the days of the horse and carts, of course. The case was filled up with this stuff and Hoppy began behaving suspiciously, making sure Mitchell saw him. Hoppy acted the part very well and

Mitchell was gloating thinking he had caught him dead to rights. He put his hand in the box and brought it out covered in manure. And there was nothing he could do about it.

§

At an NYK berth all hands were helping themselves to a bale of socks, army issue. This was the early Fifties and the money was rubbish. I believe the lads were on about nineteen shillings a day then. The ship was one of Harrison's and the socks were destined for Aden. Somehow, the police got to know and there was a blitz. About thirty or forty men on their way home at seven o'clock that evening had to get back to the ship quickly and throw the socks away. When they left the shed, the police were asking everyone to lift their trousers so they could see what kind of socks they were wearing. Some had to leave in just their boots.

§

Miss P.S., a sister in the Medical Centre at the Blue Funnel complex, was having a shower when she saw a big spider and ran out screaming for help. She grabbed the biggest docker she could find, and he went back with her to get rid of the intruder. He took one look at it and legged it! He said later he was sure she only had on green knickers under her coat …

The same woman said that was nothing compared to the time she had to go down a hatch to attend an injured docker. She had to do this by using the wooden tub, as she couldn't face the ladder. The Penguin was a first aid man and he accompanied her, but he had her a nervous wreck before they touched bottom.

§

You certainly had to keep your wits about you working in the shed, what with cranes and stackers flying all over the place, not to mention other vehicles coming and going, lorries and vans, huge articulated vehicles. Just imagine them all negotiating the restricted space in the congested sheds. You would hear someone shout a warning and instinctively you would jump and your head would try and turn 360 degrees to see where the danger was coming from. But most times it was directed at someone else further down the shed. Also, there was the added danger of being bombed by one of the many pigeons that sat on the cross-girders high above. You would have been amazed to walk into one of the sheds on the docks. Not quite as big as airplane hangars but still quite large, especially when they were filling up with cargo of every description. Wooden cases all shapes and sizes, some containing cars, tractors, machinery, pumps and compressors. These were stacked as high as the stacker or crane could reach. Reels of copper wire from BICC, rolls of barbed wire, outboard motors, huge tyres, lawnmowers, boxes of farming implements such as hoes, spades, rakes. Drums of paint, manhole covers, railway wheels. Also, pallet boards pre-stacked with every commodity under the sun. Thousands of bags – paper, hessian – containing cement, ammonium sulphate, soap powder and many more we never knew the contents of. Then there were the fine goods. These were always kept separate from this other cargo. These consisted of carpets, typewriters, crockery of all types from ordinary to bone china. Then there was the hardware. Tools of every description from chisels to power drills, wood chisels, saws, screwdrivers. Most of this stuff was stored in a corner of the shed in what they called the Cage and looked after by a watchman. Bales of cloth and boxes of the finest suiting were kept in here, as well as made-up gear. This was the stuff that attracted the pilferers, because it was easily sold, and there was a ready market for any of these items. But this area was usually surrounded by a wooden fence or wire mesh, sometimes nothing at all. Heavy wooden cases would be placed on the outside and the other stuff put in the middle. This really made me laugh. The sheds were like a supermarket actually. The only difference was they did not supply trolleys to help yourself and there were no markings on the goods to tell you what was in them. But we had a very good idea what they contained. Nine times out of ten we knew. Everything that was manufactured in the UK was brought to the docks to be exported abroad.

Outside the shed are the quays. Cargo for the ship was stored here also. Usually sheet steel, case cars, case tractors, tyres, drums of oil. Sometimes the sheet steel and other metals were placed inside the shed but not often. I remember taking away forty tons of sheet steel from one such shed; for this job we used our own tractor unit and someone else's trailer. I might add that beside the sheds and quays, there was what they called the avenue. This was quite a wide area between the sheds. Cars and buses, lorries and large cases were placed here ready for the ship. So wherever you went you saw piles of cargo.

Nothing was impregnable on the docks. Not even the Cage. This was like a prison compound, only instead of a huge, thick wall, they had mild steel mesh completely covering this area where they kept the whisky and other booze. The gates were always padlocked and usually a watchman was employed to patrol the area. But there was always a way into these enclosures. All you needed were a couple of hacksaw blades and plenty of patience and a good lookout. If they had employed younger men as watchmen, men who had better eyesight and their wits about them, it would have made stealing a lot harder. But they never learn. Most times, the artic loaded with whisky backed into the cage and there unloaded by stacker truck, but not always. Sometimes it was unloaded just outside the cage, and then there was always a chance to get a few cases, especially if the stacker driver was a thief. Not all were inclined that way, but some were. But you still had to act fast if you wanted to get any whisky; it was all split-second timing, because sometimes there would be a customs man checking the load and you had to be very careful when he was around.

I must stress that it wasn't all thieving on the docks. Most of the time we were working diligently down in the hold or on the quay. That was the beauty of the job. Each ship was different in some way; one could have MacGregor hatches, another one could have hatch-boards. It could be an old tramp, well battered, with rungs missing from the ladders going down the hatch and bent out of all proportion. Electric winches or steam; it might be taking just drums of caustic and dirty bags, or it might be taking a variety of cargo. But you took the rough with the smooth. Some jobs might be slightly boring and repetitive, but if you had good mates, you could have a laugh as you worked and make the best of it.

To get back to that locker full of whisky we raided. This was a Clan ship. The Leper, The Angry Cat, Man in a suitcase and myself were hired one morning to go to work down below. We strolled down to the ship at the bottom of the quay, near to the Vittoria Street bridge. She was high out of the water as we climbed the gangway up the ship's side. We walked aft, as we were down No. 5. The hatch-boards were already off, so we climbed down the ladder to the lower hold. Of course, I had already spotted the cage situated at the after end of the hold.

Usually the after hatch takes only general cargo, and probably dirty heavy bags, cases, barbed wire, drums, etc. ... very rarely anything of value for a bagman. This Clan ship was unique in the fact it did have a locker situated in the top tween deck. There were a few hundred tons of heavy bags also in the deck, and these stretched from the fore part of the hatch and were stacked almost up to the deck-head against the cage. The two double doors at the entrance were padlocked. And for good measure, there was a watchman in the same deck. But already my head was in overdrive on how to get at the steam. I knew the watchman could be approached, if only very carefully. Things were looking great. We climbed down to the lower hold to get the job started. It was fabulous to start at a ship expecting nothing and something like this turn up. The adrenalin started flowing. Right away I started planning with the Suitcase on our strategy. I wanted to have a nice, friendly chat with the watchman where no one could see me talking with him. Especially Mr B., the head of security. That would be fatal. I got my chance when we were climbing the trunkway to get out of the hatch. It took me about three minutes to convince him I could get it without anyone being any the wiser. I asked him did he want the cash or did he prefer bottles of whisky? He preferred the bottles. So it was all systems go. We had at least ten days to get as much as we could, providing nothing went wrong. If they put night gangs on we knew they would attempt to get into the cage. But this was the way the cookies crumbled. As it happened, three gangs were hired for the nights but, fortunately for us, they were placed down other hatches. We started the next morning, as we were first on, till 10 a.m. As soon as the trunkway mast-house was opened, I was first down and straight over to the bags. The Suitcase was right behind me. We dragged the top bag down and I climbed up quickly and surveyed the situation. A lot of bags would have to be shifted to give clear passage to the cage. I told the others to throw the other bag up right away, and I would make a start. This was done and they carried on down to the lower hold to start landing some steel. Fortunately, I would not be needed for this easy job.

I had a very hard job ahead of me, and working in a very confined space made it harder. But when there is something at the end of it, you don't mind. So I started shifting the heavy bags to one side to enable me to make a crawlspace to the cage. I can tell you, I really sweated. It took me over an hour to reach the mesh of the cage. On my way, I had to make sure that no one heard me, not that anyone would have, but Mr B. had sharp eyes and would have seen the slightest movement. I could see the watchman pacing up and down the tween deck, but I knew he couldn't see me. He knew I was in there anyway. As I said, the bags were stacked almost to the deck-head, so I was fairly well concealed. When I reached the mesh, I discovered it was rusted to hell and would present no problem. The cage wasn't completely full, but there was enough. There were quite a few different brands too. I then retraced my steps, taking care not to bang my head on the steel beams just above. I crawled out and dropped down to the deck after making sure no one could see me. I told the Suitcase we would need wirecutters. Turns out he had some metal cutters in his locker in the Pen. So after dinner we got them and we carried out the same procedure. They went below to work and I sneaked back into the bags. The cutters went through the mesh easily. I made a hole big enough for myself to climb through and dropped into the cage itself. As usual, I felt like Father Christmas in his grotto. I would have liked to have taken the whole consignment en bloc, but that was impossible. The only way we could take it was in dribs and drabs. That is, we would have to hide the bottles on our persons, and then leave the ship and walk up the quay to the Pen. So I started by taking a few cases and putting them through the hole I had made. Then I had to climb up and drag them to the other end of the bags. Some were cardboard, which was easy to rip open, but the others were made of wood and had to be broken open with the minimum of noise. This could be done with a little patience. I did manage to get them all open and took the bottles out and put them to one side, ready to be taken off the ship. I felt really happy; everything was looking good. If all went well, we would take the lot … that meant carrying off every day until the ship finished. We hoped.

There was Grant's, Johnnie Walker (Red and Black label), Cutty Sark and Vat 69. Luckily for us, the opposite gang weren't interested in it. The only one was the Angry Cat. But he wasn't greedy like us; just a few bottles would do him. I told him to keep it to himself and not to tell anyone, especially his mate, Mighty Mouse. This man was a robber like us.

The Suitcase and I started carrying the whisky from the ship to the Pen. This meant we had to first get off the ship without attracting undue attention. The people we had to look out for were crew members, and that meant ship's officers too. Also security men, and last of all, our own ship's boss. He knew what was going on and wouldn't hesitate to stop you. Once we had left the ship safely, we then had to run the gauntlet from the gangway, right to the Pen. Bear in mind we were carrying loose bottles, and it has been known for bottles to slip and fall and smash at your feet. So you had to try and walk normally if you could. On the way to the Pen, about three hundred yards away, you had to walk past all the open shed doors. The quay hands would know right away if you were carrying.

Most would give you a wink or a thumbs up. Some would ask you for a bottle. If you ignored them, you would be called a greedy bastard. At that particular ship, we gave away about forty bottles. But we were still called greedy bastards. So you cannot win. But some of the lads were genuine and would help you on your way. They would let you know if the Law was hanging around, or if any suspicious-looking characters were in the area. At the same time, your own head would be trying to turn 360 degrees. In a way, it was like playing Russian roulette each trip we made from the ship to the Pen. But I can honestly say I was never scared at any time, but the adrenalin would be flowing freely.

No one forced me to do it. I loved it. As usual, you would think all hands were watching you, but of course this was all in your mind. What makes it worse, if ever you had been pulled in the past and they thought you were at it, you could expect a pull at any time, so you were fair game, or 'open season' as the hunters would say. I had been pulled not long after I had started on the docks, but that time I hadn't stopped when they asked me, so they knew I was on the list. The Suitcase was safe enough, as he was walking behind me, about twenty yards. That was the longest walk in my life. We had to pass another Clan ship too, and if someone aboard her thought you looked bulky, they could cause trouble. It has happened. The only alternative was to walk through the huge sheds up to the Pen, but sometimes this was more hazardous. Cranes and stackers flying about all over the place, lorries shunting, and maybe a few railway wagons. And there were more places for the Law to hide too. At least if you were near the water you could empty out quick before you were grabbed. Or be like the chap on the bike who was carrying and didn't hesitate; he went straight in the dock, bike as well …

For over a week we carried off from the ship, well over five hundred bottles of whisky. As our lockers filled, we had to take so many out at a time. During this time, our lockers were attacked by the scum who didn't have the bottle (no pun intended) to carry from the ship, nor go out the gate. They used to loiter around the top floor of the Pen and listen for the clink of bottles. Even if the lockers were padlocked they used to wrench the top and bottom of the metal door, just enough to get an arm through. Even innocent men suffered from these parasites. I remember Peter L. had a brand-new suit pinched from his locker. All this just for ale money. We all knew who they were and tried not to let them know we were putting stuff in the lockers, but even that didn't help – they still robbed us.

That was my best ship for whisky. I remember chatting to the hatch boss, the Queen Mother. He knew we were helping ourselves and suggested to me that we had had enough! 'When the locker's empty,' I replied. I even offered to get him some bottles, but he refused, saying, 'I wouldn't have that rubbish in the house, I have only the best …' I nearly fell about laughing. The stuff we had taken was of some of the finest brands. To give him his due, he wouldn't have taken anything that was stolen. Of course, we gave the little old watchman about ten bottles of Johnnie Walker, and he was more than happy. No one got drunk that time and everything went smoothly. I knew men who had caused the watchman to be sacked just because they didn't give a monkey's.

Of course, we had men from other hatches sniffing around asking for handouts ... we just said it was impossible to get at and the watchman was a bastard. But they never believed us. That was a very happy ship for me. You mustn't forget that we also worked at loading the ship as well as taking the whisky off; we didn't just spend all our time taking the whisky. Of course, there were times when the job didn't necessitate all four men being on.

§

Two Pakistani gentlemen arrived at a certain dock in Liverpool, each driving a car. These were to be shipped back to India. It was their bad luck that the checker they entrusted them to was bent. After they were given directions to Lime Street station and they had left, both cars were driven from the dock and sold.

§

Two very expensive greyhounds were delivered to a certain dock to be shipped out. But a certain docker who came to work on the mini shift later left with them both on leads, straight out of the gate.

§

Way back in 1947, a large Mercedes Benz was being winched aboard a Henderson ship. It was en route to the Yugoslav Embassy in India. As the winch was hoisting it up, it scraped the shed wall and was damaged. When it was examined properly, the wing was found to be made of gold! It turned out the gold was being smuggled out of England in this unique way. I cannot vouch for this tale, but no doubt older dockers may recall it.

§

A holdsman borrowed a Rolls-Royce that was going abroad. He went for a few drinks to Blowers up Limekiln Lane but had too much to drink and crashed on the way back. Another man, a crane driver, took a Mercedes Benz from Lewis's Quay, filled it with a few cases of whisky and took the lot out to sell. He was full of drink himself and was very lucky to get away with it.

§

We were working on a Clan Line ship on days. Little Jock, the watchman, was standing on the deck looking down at us on the quay. A few minutes earlier we had managed to get half a dozen TV sets off a pallet board that was going in the ship, and to hide them to take out later. We had hidden ours and watched Big A. scurrying along in the shed trying to find a good hiding place for the TV he was carrying. God knows why he bothered, because he had no transport to take it out. Also, we knew Little Jock had seen him and was about to sound the alarm. The annoying thing was Jock was watching the whisky at another hatch, but he wouldn't hesitate to blow you up if he saw you misbehaving. Big A. got a little nervous when he heard this, so I offered to go and see Jock and tell him the TV would be returned (he didn't know about ours though) if he didn't call the police. So I went aboard the ship and had a word with him. Surprisingly enough, he agreed to say nothing if the TV was put back. This itself was unusual because normally he was a pure bastard.

§

Jackie T., a hatch boss, was on nights at No. 3 Duke, near to Ranks Mills. The ship's boss was giving him his orders during the day, but Jackie was not taking too much notice because he was quite drunk. The boss was not aware of this. He pointed to a pile of steel on the quay, over 200 tons that had to be taken aboard the ship that night. This was duly done. Or so they thought. By mistake, Jackie had picked the wrong pile. The steel he had sent in was specially made and painted white for Ranks to build a canopy. So it all had to come out of the hatch.

§

We were working days on the North Quay on a Harrison ship, and the shed was bursting at the seams with cargo. J.D. and I discovered some heavy wooden cases containing about six ton of cupronickel. Before we took it we decided to get a portion analysed to make sure it was what we thought. It was. The cases were very heavy and about 6 feet in length. We then had to get a crane to drag them almost the full length of the shed, from one end to the other and near the door at No. 1 hatch for it to be picked up by the dockside crane and onto the trailer we had borrowed for the occasion. I can add that the ship's boss, Les N., unfortunately caught us in the middle of operations. And he wasn't soft either. He knew what was going on. After some hasty explaining, he agreed to look the other way. I promised him a small remuneration for his co-operation. He couldn't have done anything anyway, because we had plenty of excuses and there would be absolutely no chance of any comeback for myself and J.D. It was really as bad or as good as that on the docks. Unless you were actually caught red-handed doing something illegal, you could put two fingers up. As I have said, you could get away with murder practically. Anyway, the boss snarled for a few minutes and then took off in the opposite direction very quickly. We then proceeded to organise the crane and trailer and did the business. We did have a little bother with the crane driver, who went for his tea and it was during his absence we did the business. I think he was the Rocket Man, but he was soon told the facts of life. He was afraid of getting involved, but he was in the clear absolutely. Ridiculous how some people go to pieces when the police are mentioned. That little caper came off quite successfully and, as promised, the boss got his handout.

Once, Joey B. was carrying a few bottles of whisky around his waist as he pedalled his way out of the dock on his bike. But as he turned the corner of the shed to head for the gate, he saw the police had blocked the road off and were stopping everyone. We used to call this a blitz, when the Law swooped like this. He was practically on top of them before he realised. But his brain must have gone into overdrive at that moment. With lightning-fast reflexes, he turned sharp left and headed for the water and went straight in, bike and all ... I was right behind him on my scooter at the time, also carrying bottles of whisky. Talk about the Key-Stone cops ... they all chased him to the water's edge and allowed me to go through unmolested. It was very hairy, but it happened so fast. I glanced quickly at the scene and got away fast. In the meanwhile, my saviour was treading water and smashing the bottles below the surface. The boys in blue lined the quay wall, telling him to get out and not do anything foolish – the game was up. After he had destroyed the evidence, our swimmer got out looking like a drowned rat and was promptly arrested and put in the back of a police Land Rover. Of course, there wasn't any evidence, and they had to let him go. They asked him why he had pedalled into the dock, and he replied he just felt like a dip. 'What about your bike?' they countered. He just shrugged and said he had completely forgotten about it. Of course, they sent a police diver down to try and locate the evidence, but it was a complete waste of time. I suppose they could have done him for dumping his bike in the dock, but I don't suppose they ever even thought about it. So there was a good example of a man keeping his mouth shut and denying every accusation they threw at him and getting away with it. J.B. went on the list after that escapade.

§

The Penguin was working on the quay on nights, with some Liverpool men, at a Clan ship. They were using what they call 'dogs' to pick up some very heavy wooden cases and place them on a net board. Dogs are a simple device consisting of two pieces of iron triangular in shape with a flat part consisting of sharp pointed teeth, which dig into the wood. There are two and they are joined through eyes by a length of rope. When the crane takes the weight, you are supposed to hold the dogs until the teeth dig in. But now and again accidents will happen and one dog will fly off and catch the unwary docker. This is what happened to a Liverpool docker; it caught him just over his eye, opening up a gash and the blood just cascaded out. The Penguin was qualified to give first aid, but the man needed hospital treatment and stitches. An ambulance was called, and the injured man was taken aboard accompanied by the Penguin. At casualty, the doctor asked him to wait outside. Then he started to ask some particulars from the injured man.

'How did it happen?' he asked.

'One of the dogs flew off the case and hit me.'

The doctor looked a little confused by this statement.

'What do you mean a dog hit you? You mean it bit you?'

'No, I was holding my dog and the Talking Horse was holding the other one, but he let go too soon and it came off and got me.'

The doctor looked perplexed and thought the man was suffering from concussion. He checked his eyes and found he was OK. The docker thought he could help and said, 'Look doc, if you don't believe me, just go outside and ask the Penguin. He was there, and Harry the Birdman …' Exit one very confused doctor.

§

We were working nights at a Norwegian ship in Liverpool. A couple of the girls were aboard parading around wearing next to nothing. They were available to anyone who could pay. We were all sitting in a mess room aft during the welt. The Cisco Kid was lusting after one of them. 'I wouldn't mind giving her one,' he said to me. I told him to be very careful because the Norwegians could turn nasty.

'Besides,' he said, 'if I ask her, where could we do it?'

'What's wrong with right here in the mess room?' I replied.

He looked at me in disbelief. 'You a fuckin' voyeur or something?'

I laughed at him. 'Where's your sense of humour, and don't forget one important thing …'

He looked at me enquiringly. 'What?' he asked.

'Your brother-in-law is sitting over there. Aren't you scared he'll blow you up to your missus?'

Just then, the girl came over and sat on his knee. I could see he was getting all steamed up and noticed his brother-in-law watching. But the romance was over quickly as a large Norwegian came in and picked her up bodily and carried her off to his cabin. They were both the worse for wear. I consoled him somewhat by saying, 'Look at it this way Kid, it could have been a trip to a certain Dr Ross [he specialised in venereal disease] or at least a dose of Sandy McNabs [crabs].' He didn't find it funny, but we broke up laughing.

§

'Would you pass me that piece of wood?' Alec asked the Leper.

The Leper did so and then was promptly threatened with it. He asked Alec why he was behaving in such a way.

'Because your fuckin' mate promised me some shirts and didn't give me any ...'

'So what's that got to do with me?' asked the Leper.

'Because he's your fuckin' mate, that's why.'

The Leper didn't know whether to laugh or get a shrink down the hatch, because this wasn't normal behaviour.

It turned out the Fugitive was down another hatch and had the shirts going. He had come up on deck, looked over the rail onto the quay, saw Alec and asked him if the coast was clear. That was all. Somehow Alec had got it into his head he had been employed as a watchman. Strange man.

§

Paddy M. was sent from the Pen one morning to a South African ship at No. 1 Duke. A few hours later he was reported missing. He was seen in Joney's paper shop hanging around. The owner became a little suspicious and watched him. One of the lads came in and asked Paddy what he was doing there. Then it dawned on everyone and he was directed to the ship. Another time, the same man was sent to the Bidston Dock but somehow finished over in the Gladstone Dock in Liverpool.

§

My early days on Birkenhead docks I remember very well. Certain incidents remain fresh in my memory, like watching various men helping themselves to broached cargo. I watched one man, Billy C., stuffing his pockets with tubes of toothpaste. He put them in every recess he could find, even some in his socks. He saw me watching him and started laughing. 'Why don't you help yourself, Len?' he asked.

At that time I just wasn't interested and told him so. He just laughed again and said, 'Good, that leaves more for me.' I thought it was rather silly to get caught and lose your job just for a few shillings. But shortly afterwards I started helping myself. Funny thing is I never got pulled once, but once I got known I couldn't go out the gate without being asked to stop and be searched. The time came when I just couldn't leave any ship without taking something. Men had been caught with ridiculous things like toothpaste, a bar of chocolate, even dry tea from the hold. Even to be caught with a few bottles of gin or whisky was bad enough. I even knew a man who took out cartons of Tampax; the mind boggles at that! You would be asked to step inside a dockside police hut to be searched, but not always – sometimes they would do it in a shed or on the quay, anywhere. You could object to this and demand to be searched in private. But most of the lads put up with it rather than create a fuss. But it was a bit much in front of a busload of people gawking out of the windows. I know men who lost their jobs through being caught with a few sweets taken from the hatch.

Steve K., a holdsman, took some Dundee cake that was being exported out of the hatch. He ate a lot and decided to take some home. He was stopped on the quay by the police and was searched, whereupon they found the cake. He had to attend Court and he was fined £50 but fortunately he didn't lose his job. When he booked on for work the next day, all his mates were there and started singing, 'If we knew you were coming, we'd have baked a cake.'

We all make mistakes at one time or another. And you are supposed to learn from them. One of my own big mistakes was trusting too many people. One person caused my incarceration. I relied too much on him, and he let me down. I blame myself for this.

§

You would be down below stowing whisky in the locker under the watchful eyes of a watchman and maybe a cadet officer. A sling would come in and the smell of whisky would be extra strong, which meant a bottle was broken, maybe a few bottles. We called these leakers. Accidents will happen, either on the quay or down below. In a case like this, all hands frantically start looking for something to catch the escaping whisky. You wouldn't get much, but at least enough to whet your appetite. They didn't object to you doing this; at least they never said so. The whisky came in either wooden cases or cardboard. It was well packed, but there were still ways you could manage to do some damage and get yourself a drink. For instance, a wooden case could be dropped down point first onto another one and break the flimsy protection, and it would splinter easily. Then you just helped yourself, keeping your eye on the watchman all the time. He would probably have his eye on you all the time too, but if you were determined enough, you could do it. I have been in a locker with two watchmen and a cadet and still managed to get a few bottles. Maybe while you are waiting for a sling to come in or if you stayed on while the other gang worked, you might do it. I always carried a sharp blade to get through the cardboard case easily with my back to the pile. Takes some doing, acting as if you're leaning against it without the watchman tumbling. But it was done as long as you had a bit of patience. If you are seen and warned, you must obey. I never threatened a watchman ever; didn't have to. I was warned a few times, and I just accepted it. Why threaten and frighten an old man who's only trying to do his job?

I even remember a stacker driver ramming his forks into the whisky just so we could get some. I sure was glad I wasn't paying for some of the damage caused down below. It was all placed squarely on the Insurance people, who we reckoned are the biggest thieves in the world. I used to wince at some of the damage that was deliberate. And the wastage too was something to be seen. Imagine a docker opening a box of chocolate, selecting the nuts and then throwing the rest down the stringers. When he was asked why, he replied, 'I only like the hard ones, don't like the rest.' Or drinking the juice out of a tin of pears or pineapples and then dumping the rest. We certainly wouldn't have done it if we had to pay for it.

Some ships we got to know quite well with working on them several times. Like how to get into the locker to attack the whisky. We always looked out for the weak spots. When I think of the antics grown men would get up just to get at the hard stuff, it amazes me still. I include myself in this category. The one thing I never did was stay the night down the hatch when everyone else has gone home. But I would have done it if it had been worthwhile. The beauty of this was that you could get everything ready for the next morning to carry off without the watchman knowing. I have known men climb down ventilators to get at the goodies. A few men have fallen and had nasty accidents while attempting to steal in a darkened hatch, especially when they were not working at that particular ship. I know of two men who did this and were very lucky to be alive. Like that one man who fell into the lower hold and had to be got out by his friends and placed on the quay to make it look like the accident took place there. I don't know why it happened, because whenever I did something similar, I always carried a torch, small but powerful enough to see what was going on. We always had tools in our lockers for the different jobs we came across: drills, saws, hammers, bars, metal cutters, spare locks. If you are going to do it, do it properly. The only thing we didn't use was dynamite. Sometimes we used primitive methods to get a door off a locker for a one-off. This method was crude but very effective. The runner was lowered from the winch and hooked up to the door and simply heaved off bodily. Then you had to grab what you wanted quickly and as many as you could before the security arrived. Only did this once. Never liked this method. Far better to remove the lock and replace it with a similar one of your own and hope they wouldn't look too closely. If they did, all would be up. But nine times out of ten, we got away with it. You could empty a locker nice and steady this way, and we would have done several times, but time is against you, because it's a slow process getting into a locker, concealing it on your person and then getting out and making your way from the ship. You could be climbing out of the hatch, for instance, and when you reached the deck, you had to climb over the coaming, making sure the bottles didn't fall out and smash, thereby drawing attention to you. The worst thing that could happen was when the lads started to drink the stuff when it was going. Spoiled a few good jobs when that happened. They say, 'Just one drink, that's all I want. Where's the harm?' So they have their drink and that's followed by more and it's going down very easily. And straight from the bottle. Cutty Sark, 100 Pipers, Johnny Walker (Black and Red Label), Grant's. It was all the same. They drank it just like it was water, and there was hell to pay later. The poor watchman would be having a coronary because he would be in trouble for allowing it. The poor bastard had no choice really. There weren't many who would stand up to a huge docker and tell him to stop. After a few drinks, the songs would start and then all hands would think they were at the London Palladium or the Sands in Vegas. Or one particular chap I remember thought he was at the La Scala in front of a Milanese audience, and he would give out with *Largo al factotum* from *The Barber of Seville*. The Leper, alias Danny Kaye – here was a fine example of a man wanting to have just one gargle to clear the throat. Fatal. Man in a Suitcase and I had a good thing going at one of Brock's – quart bottles of gin (Beefeater) and Johnny Walker (Black Label). Paradise. Or so we thought. Even the watchman was on our side. What could be better? The Suitcase and I started carrying the bottles off good style, making a good start. We were loading the whisky down the deep tanks, so we had plenty of opportunity to fill our boots. I never did like carrying those quart bottles, as they are so bulky. But as the man said, 'You're not bothering then?' Just as if I never refused anything. I always said anyone that doesn't work the welt or carry off is arse ... this always got a laugh. Anyway, we were making good progress until Suitcase and I were on our way back to the ship for another load, when we were met by a friend who warned us that the customs were all over the place and down our hatch, and also our good friend the Leper was lying in the avenue, out of the game. We knew then that the worst had happened and we made our way quickly to the scene. Sure enough, there was the Leper lying among some dunnage on the deck in the avenue. He was out. I got my car ready, but we couldn't get him in, as he was too heavy and awkward, so we finished up calling a taxi. The driver wasn't too pleased at the state of the Leper, but we assured him he wouldn't throw up.

We took him home and carried him up two flights of stairs. How we cursed him for putting the blocks on all our efforts. We were calling him all sorts of a bastard for getting drunk, but our words fell on deaf ears. He was coming out with all sorts of gibberish, and he was trying to sing as we got him to his front door, but his brain was out of sync with his voice. So much for just a gargle. It's fatal when the lads start drinking it. I only did it once, but that particular time I wasn't taking any off the ship because most of the lads were drunk and the police were on the quay.

One of the best ways of getting the whisky before it went into the cage or locker in the ship was to waylay it. There were a number of ways you could do this. One was during the journey from the locker in the shed on the quay to the shed doorway near the hatch which was taking the whisky. When the stacker truck picked up the pallet board full of whisky for the trip to the shed doorway it was usually watched all the way to stop pilfering. But there were ways around this. A diversion would be created such as a crane blocking the view for a few seconds, but you had to be very quick to snatch a couple of cases and hide them. And just as quickly you had to make sure the load looked intact by rearranging the cases. Another way was for the stacker to have a minor collision, thus spilling the load, causing a little confusion during which time more cases would disappear quickly. This works better when there is a pallet board already at the stage end ready to go aboard the ship. You would get some co-operation from the deckhand to slow down a little (if the boss wasn't near and watching); if he was, you had no chance, because he was always chasing the job up. You had to watch the ship's officers and crew members as well. The whole operation takes a few minutes and again success depends on luck as well. You could be in the middle of doing the business and suddenly it is jeopardised by the appearance of a police van coming through the shed or a ship's officer coming on deck and standing by the hatch to watch proceedings. But these things happen now and again. It's just the luck of the draw. You win some and you lose some. Another way we got the whisky was when it actually went into the hatch. Here again you had to have a co-operative crane driver and a lot of luck. There would be a watchman standing on the deck near the hatch, and if he didn't go to the coaming and watch the pallet board go down, you had a chance, or also if the watchman down below wasn't looking up. The pallet board would come over and the driver would slow down near the tween deck giving the men waiting there just time enough to grab a few cases and hide them. It was all luck really. Everything had to go your way when the time came for the snatch. It was pure magic when everything went smoothly and the watchmen and security were none the wiser. As long as the lads didn't start drinking it.

I can remember one amusing incident when we were trying very hard to get some whisky but the odds were against us because we had a bad watchman on the quay at the gate where J.D. and I were hooking on together. We happened to be working on the quay at this Clan ship and they started loading whisky. Little J., the watchman, was standing near us and watching like a hawk, so we had no chance. Plus there was a watchman on the deck of the ship looking down at us. We could have got a couple of bottles by cutting the cardboard case and getting them that way but we didn't want to do this. We wanted a few cases. But you never knew what turned up most of the time, and you just bided your time and hoped for the best. Sure enough, something happened, and we took full advantage of it. The stacker was bringing the whisky from the locker down at the other end of the shed roughly three hundred yards away. Suddenly, we heard a commotion and looked down toward the locker and saw the stacker had collided with some cases, spilling most of his load. The shed floor was strewn with cases of whisky. We couldn't leave our job anyway, so there was no chance of us going down. We already had a pallet board full of whisky waiting for the crane on the quay. The watchman, Little J., made a bad mistake here; he was so worried about the whisky all over the floor that he left us and went down the shed to make sure no one helped themselves to the cases all over the deck. We just couldn't believe it at first, but after we had got over the surprise, we got stuck in at the whisky under our feet. A quick glance at the ship to make sure no one was watching us and we got stuck in rapidly. Even if someone had been watching, it would have made no difference; we wouldn't have stopped. Luckily, the Amenity Block was about a hundred yards away, so J.D. and I made off up the quay with a case of whisky each. Quickly stowing the bottles in our lockers, we got back to the ship and grabbed another case each. We did the same again, putting the bottles in our lockers to be taken out later. We were leaving the building to return to our job when we saw Arthur D. standing near the water's edge at the bows of the ship. We strolled over to see what the commotion was about and saw our friend J.B. in the water. It was getting on for winter, so it wasn't too hot for him. I got a gall wire quickly, and when he grabbed hold, we pulled him out. I will never forget seeing his face looking up at us and saying, 'Get me out, Lenny.' There were no steps near where he'd gone in, so we had to pull him out. Then we got him into the showers quickly and a change of clothes and he was as good as new. J.D. and I then learned what had happened. It was incredible. For some reason, J.B. and A.D. decided to commandeer a stacker truck and put two cases of whisky on it and started to make their way to the Amenity Block. But they never made it because J.B., who was driving, lost control for some reason, and with A.D. sitting on it, it headed straight for the water. The next day they had to get a diver down to recover the stacker-truck. They never recovered the cases of whisky that went to the bottom. What a fiasco that was.

§

The lads were loading whisky and were feeling very thirsty, so they asked the watchman if they could have a gargle. 'No chance,' he replied. 'Touch that whisky and I'll blow you up.' So they knew where they stood then. No amount of soft soap would make him change his mind. He wouldn't give in to their pleadings. But he did say if by chance any breakages came in they could have the drips. Big deal. Pallet after pallet came in and no luck. All hands were very unhappy at this state of affairs until the relief stacker driver came on. The first thing he asked was, 'Let's have a drink to make me happy. Who's got the bottle?' He was told what had happened. The driver, the Red Baron, said he would alter those circumstances immediately. Whereupon he jumped onto his stacker and rammed the steel forks into a longer of whisky. All hands dived for cups and such like to stem the flow of leaking whisky.

Another time, Deaf Billy was on days at Harrison's on the Golden Mile. Whisky flowing down the scuppers and all hands were very happy. It got so bad that all work stopped and the lads were threatened by the boss. The timekeeper was called to the scene and was promptly told to fuck off. Eventually, the police were called to try and sort it all out. They were threatened and one actually was thrown over the side into the water. The police radioed for reinforcements, and the situation was brought under control. The watchman was sacked right away.

§

At F Troop there was a watchman who was dead keen and conscientious and wouldn't let them have a go at the whisky. However, the lads managed to make a sizeable hole in the mesh of the cage and helped themselves. The poor watchman discovered it and promptly fainted!

Another ploy used by the lads in F Troop was to carry a dead rat with them to each ship they worked on. They would then use the rat as evidence for the shop steward to get a few extra shillings because of the risk involved. It was called rat infestation.

§

Big Alf and Sammy M. were on nights at the Clan. They made a tunnel through the cargo consisting of lavatory pans in wooden skeleton frameworks. We used to load hundreds of these. They had to go through this cargo to get at the whisky. It was hard work shifting all those articles but they made good progress. Suddenly, Big Alf cried out that he was trapped and couldn't go any further. Turned out he had his foot jammed down one of the lavatory pans. So the expedition had to be cancelled to try and extricate him. There was no space to put the pans to one side out of the way, but after a lot of hard work, they finally got him out and the burrowing went on with great success.

§

Occasionally, there was no work here in Birkenhead, not because there weren't any ships in, but simply because all the ships were completely manned and there was a surplus of dockers. In this case, we sometimes went over to Liverpool to help out with the discharging. Personally, I never cared for it. But sometimes we enjoyed the outing. I have some happy memories working at the Gladstone with the Leper, Man in a

Suitcase and the Angry Cat. We would take a walk through the shed and help ourselves to the best of tinned food. For dinner, we enjoyed John West middle-cut salmon, maybe a couple of tins, followed by a tin of pears or fruit cocktail or peaches. Large tins of course. We had bread ready for the salmon and a fork and spoon. We would sit on the dock wall and eat like pigs in the hot sun, watching the ships passing up and down the river. Great days. If our luck was out and we couldn't help ourselves to the stuff in the shed, we would leg it up to Eboes Café on Regent Road and fill up on egg and chips or partake of his famous rissole butties with piccalilli. How I enjoyed these. I believe they made coffins at the rear of his premises. Certainly didn't put anyone off their food.

On one occasion, the Penguin was on the quay at a ship discharging boxes of tea in Liverpool. Bert K. was his real name. Lived in Birkenhead. I knew him personally. A sling came over from the ship and tilted slightly as it was landed on the bogie. A couple of cases fell onto Bert and he went down for the count. A Liverpool docker, not knowing his real name, ran to the gate and informed the policeman on duty to get an ambulance as the Penguin was hurt. The policeman, not knowing Burt, rang the RSPCA and they came down instead. The driver jumped out demanding to know where the injured Penguin was … red faces all round.

One day he was standing on the quay alongside the fishing boat that was selling fish to the lads. He wanted to buy some, so he shouted down to a crewman, who promptly asked did he want the fish wrapped or should he throw them up to him so he could catch them in his mouth. Bert was not amused.

Another time, he was involved in an argument with another quay hand and it got quite heated. They were going at it hammer and tongs when someone else butted in and said to both of them, 'Why don't you forget it and make up?' Bert agreed until the other man said, 'OK, let's forget it, and shake on it. Give us your flipper …'

§

There was nothing like heading down to the docks to start work. Especially if you knew it was going to be laughs all the way. This all depended on who you were working with. They had to have the same sense of humour or something similar. Imagine a friend greeting you one morning and telling you he had seen your wife or girlfriend coming off a Greek ship at 8 a.m. Not many could accept it. You certainly had to have a thick skin to work down there. No room for the fainthearted or sensitive type. Even going down the ladder to the lower hold you weren't safe. Someone would be trying to step on your fingers. No good complaining. You would be called a fuckin' cissy or a big baby. Anyone who wore gloves was arse. I always wore them, so took a load of insults. I wouldn't work without them anyway.

'Who the fuck do you think you are? A fuckin' brain surgeon?'

'Fuckin' big tart ...'

'Where's this case goin'?'

'Not up your arse anyway ... where the fuck do you think it's goin'? Go 'ed, have three guesses. Down the fuckin' funnel, in the Captain's cabin or maybe its goin' in the chain locker?'

Eventually the case would be stowed in its proper place.

Simple little things would sometimes erupt into a full discussion, and the participants would get very heated. All in good fun. There was never any bitterness between us. It helped pass the time away down below, but the time went fairly quickly anyway. If anyone wanted to go anywhere especially, it would have been arranged between us somehow. It all depended on the particular job we were on at the time. We used to get away with murder at times. Sometimes when you were down below you would have to wait while the quay hands found the cargo required. They could have had a difficult job trying to extricate it from among other cases; they might have had to shift other cargo to get at it. All this takes time, of course, and while they could be struggling on the quay, we would have to wait. We could spend this time just sitting or lying down on some cases resting. Or someone would start asking questions on general knowledge. This could take in a variety of subjects from horse racing, movies, pop music, world affairs, politics, anything under the sun. Or if there were any cases that we had stowed looked interesting someone would go over with a bar or hook and start attacking it just to see what was inside it.

§

A little story about one of the deep tanks we were working down for about four days. The day came when it was completed. We had filled it with general cargo. Drums, bags, cases, probably worth around twenty thousand pounds. We all got out of the tank and stood around for a few minutes watching the huge steel lid being lifted in place, and the heavy nuts being screwed on. One of our colleagues who had been working down the tank with us, a certain Silver Bullet, definitely not a candidate for Mastermind, asked a good question.

'Do they fill it up with water now?'

I had the misfortune to work with him and another man famous for non-exertion. This character always had a cigarette hanging out the corner of his mouth. Needless to say, the inch-long ash never fell off. The Bullet's hands were welded to the insides of his pockets. His feet were used to propel the cargo. Imagine trying to stow huge Stanton pipes with these two. At that time, there were only the three of us keeping the job going. Enough said.

§

Billy M. and Tommy B. and Nick the Greek were on their way home from Liverpool after working at a grain ship. As they came out of the tunnel, someone suggested a drink in the Park View pub, near the docks. They were sitting there having a quiet drink but Nick the Greek was spoiling it by swearing a lot, turning the air blue. Every other word was 'fuck this', 'fuck that'. Billy and Tommy were getting hot under the collar as the barmaid was close by, and asked him to tone it down.

Nick was highly indignant. 'She knows the fuckin' score; she fuckin' hears a lot worse in here.'

Tommy asked him how did it affect his kids at home. Nick was surprised at this question.

'They swear fuckin' worse than me,' he answered.

§

I have nothing but the greatest admiration for these men. As I have said, I have had a number of jobs doing all sorts, but I can honestly say I have never known such a great crowd of men. I could never attempt to remember all their names because there were a few thousand. Faces, yes, and maybe nicknames. Sadly, I hear that a lot of them have passed away since I have left. I know a lot of them served in the army and merchant navy during the Second World War because I used to talk to them about it. And you had to drag it out of them, because they never spoke about it.

One quay hand I remember told me he was sunk while he was still in the engine room of a tramp steamer with a young deck boy who survived also. They were the only ones to do so. He was actually in the tunnel which contains the prop shaft when it happened.

Deaf Billy told me about a Commie boat he was working on one time and they were loading steel coils of wire. These are very awkward to manhandle at any time and dangerous. Like railway wheels, they have to be rolled into the wings just like a kid's hoop. They would come in the hatch two or three at a time and were supposed to be landed against some kind of a support. Wooden tubs were mainly used for this purpose. Billy said they didn't have anything at that time, but the management promised to get something as soon as possible. In the meanwhile, the lads carried on as best as they could. Two men would hold the coils steady while a third man unhooked the gall wire and pulled it clear. Then you have to start rolling the coils into the wings. A coil started to fall over and the men scattered quickly, but Billy wasn't quick enough and the coil scraped down his legs and fell on his feet. If it weren't for his steel toecaps, he would have lost some of his toes. He was off work for a short time and was awarded £500 for his troubles. If they had worked by the book, it probably would never have happened. Here is a fine example of the much-maligned docker doing a job of work which no factory would even think of doing.

§

J.W., a small chap with a giant-sized chip on his shoulder, was stopped by a large policeman on the gate. Full outfit. Blue serge, silver buttons and numbers on his shoulder, blue shirt, dark tie. He wanted to search J.W., who was very indignant and demanded to see the policeman's identification.

'How do I know you are a policeman?' he asked.

§

W.O. left the dock with two bottles of whisky concealed on him and was feeling very happy until a police Land Rover pulled up alongside him on the dock road. He promptly filled his trousers with excreta through fear. He was sacked as well, poor man.

§

I was taking a small sample of metal out one day to get it analysed to see if it was worth anything. A certain policeman who was known as a good runner stopped me. I had to empty my pockets in the hut as usual and he picked up this sample and my adrenalin started pumping. He wanted to know what it was and where did I get it. I told him I had seen it lying on the floor in the shed and had picked it up out of curiosity. Actually, I had taken it from a drum in the shed. Technically, he could have charged me with stealing, because taking anything from the dock estate is forbidden. But after a few minutes, he accepted my story and let me go. If he had only known that sample was part of a cargo of a precious metal, six tons in all, which we took later and sold. I think it was called Molybdenum. Even if you took some firewood home to start your fire (those days have gone forever), you were guilty of stealing from the dockyard even though there was tons of scrap wood lying about all over the place. I never made that mistake again, but I am getting ahead of myself here in forgetting the biggest, silliest mistake ever, but I shall tell about that further on. It was my closest shave ever.

§

When a large ship comes alongside to load cargo, it has to be secured to the quay, using thick ropes and sometimes wires known as springs. In between the ship and the quay are found huge deals of timber and plenty of old thick tyres bunched together. These are used as a buttress to protect the quay wall and the ship's side. Huge nets are slung from the bulwarks down to the quay and secured. These are safety nets to stop any falling cargo going into the water. Or they might use large boards in the same way. Some of us used to leave the ship using these boards, throw a rope over and climb down to the quay. Strictly forbidden, of course. The nets did come in handy sometimes for stopping human cargo from going into the water – men who had been celebrating too much.

It could be very dangerous working in a hold, especially when the crane or winch was bringing in the cargo. You had to remember all the time you were down there never to walk out into the square without first looking up. Hard hats were not even thought of then. Your mate could be in the top or lower tween deck throwing slabs or dunnage down to be used with the cargo. A lump of wood on your skull would do as much damage as a netboard full of drums if it hit you. I remember a friend, J.D., completely forgetting and walking out from cover in the lower hold and a small drum fell from a pallet board and smashing into the deck inches from him! That was a very close call.

Working on the quay could be just as dangerous. Cranes and stacker trucks flying about all over the place. I seldom worked on the quay in a gang. There would be five men to a hatch. One man would be at the fall to hook on the cargo, he was called the stage-end man. Sometimes he was nailed there for most of the day; it all depended on the cargo and the men he worked with. The other four men would split up into pairs and they would still work the welt between them, and when the occasion arose, they would let the stage-end go for his break at the canteen. If, for example, the two men were picking up bags and the crane driver was taking them to the hatch, one of the two men would go back to the fall and hook on, but this just did not happen very often. Certain bad jobs, like bags off the deck, meant the stage-end man was stuck with it until the job changed and we went onto pallet boards with pre-packed items. Then one gang would give him a break by hooking on, which really needed two men, one either side to slip the bars under the pallet boards. A lot of men were selfish and didn't give a damn about the poor old stage-end; it was just tough luck for him, but at the same time, he could have it cushy just hooking on while his mates were on a backbreaking job picking up bags and placing them on boards.

I can only remember being on the stage-end once and that was enough. But it was interesting working in the sheds at times. The cases would be stacked up on top of each other like multi-storey flats. They had to go high so as to save space. Cranes or stackers were used to do all this work. These drivers deserved all the praise going for working under extremely difficult circumstances. Space was restricted at most times, but somehow they managed. This was a most responsible job they had to do, as the cargo had to be stowed safely because others were working around it. When they had to take something to the hatch – for example, long pipes – a man would be required to guide it through the shed, through all the narrow confines and awkward corners. Sometimes the driver had to lower his jib and drag the cargo along the floor, especially the older sheds with low wooden beams. I often saw the cab of the crane tipping as it went along dragging a heavy load to the ship's side. But it had its humorous moments too. Like the time Tommy S. was driving a crane with a large heavy case on the hook with a quay hand holding onto the case and guiding him through the shed. Tommy clipped a huge pile of corn flake cartons piled sky high and shouted a warning to his helper. The poor man panicked, put his head down and ran. Straight into the wooden case and knocked himself out. He was off for six months with some dislocated vertebrae in his neck. The irony was the corn flakes wouldn't have hurt him at all.

§

On the night shift at Gladstone Dock, a crane driver with a weird sense of humour somehow took possession of a tailor's dummy and had it in his cab of the crane high above the dockside shed. He dressed it in some old clothes complete with a cheese-cutter (hat). There were some men on the deck of the ship including the deckhand who is passing the word to him. Suddenly, the crane driver stands up at the cab window and shouts down (as if he has suddenly cracked up), 'I've had enough of this. I can't take any more.' All hands look up to see this figure hurtling through the window and heading for the quayside. Everyone was horrified at this sight; the hatch boss nearly had a heart attack.

Another crane driver was working on a crane called *Jonathan*. This was a real museum piece and the cab was about six or seven feet from the ground. It had solid tyres and was extremely difficult to manage. However, Davy C. had a go. But one day he forgot he was so far off the ground and stepped out. So he had to spend a few weeks in hospital.

§

Men were sitting eating their lunch at the dockside canteen at dinnertime. Some brought their own butties consisting of many ingredients: bacon, ham and tomato, salmon, jam, marmalade, egg. Smoke was thick overhead. Talk was incessant. Even with a mouthful of food, a man would be arguing, spraying food on anyone nearby. No room for decorum here. The worst thing that could happen was if someone broke wind while we were all eating. But incredibly, we all thought it was hilarious. Of course, some blue-blood would think it really disgusting (which it was really) and complain. 'Ya dirty bastard.' Naturally, the guilty man would deny it and blame someone else.

The conversation at the next table was getting really heated.

'Fuck off,' sneered Lurch, 'Hagler was the best middle-weight ever.'

The Leper just smiled. 'Obviously you know fuck all about boxing.'

'Ever hear of Sugar Ray Robinson? Try looking at all his fights and you will see, after you've had an eye test, that Robinson was the best pound for pound middle-weight of all time.'

Lurch wouldn't have it. 'What about Leonard then?'

'What about him?' said the Leper. 'He wouldn't have lasted four rounds.'

'What about Basilio then?'

'He was good, very good. But not good enough for Robinson.'

'That's only your opinion, Leper.'

'Of course, but the man's record speaks for itself. He was simply the best there ever was …'

The Angry Cat butted in. 'So you say, but how do you know?'

'The Leper just smiled 'Stick to movies, Cat, and you're on safe ground. Boxing is not your metier … why do you people go on about something you don't know anything about?'

'Here ya then, fuckin' knowall … who played Kitty in the TV series *Gunsmoke*?' This was snarled by the Angry Cat. His face would be twisted in a grimace and his glasses would be all steamed up.

The Leper would be smiling. 'Why don't you fuckin' ask us something hard? Any soft bastard knows that.'

'Go on then, tell me, ya don't fuckin' know. Who was it?'

'If I tell you, will you think I'm just the greatest?'

The Cat would be almost foaming at the mouth. All hands would be doubled up with laughing. 'Go on then, who was it?'

The Leper: 'I'm not sayin' …'

Big Alby butts in. 'Here ya then, I've got one for ya. Who was the first man sent off in the World Cup series?'

'Fuck off, Alby, it's not your turn,' said the Cat. 'Answer my question first …'

'What was the question?'

'You won't fuckin' know anyway. Stick to ya football …'

'Fuck off, ya twat, who the fuck d'ya think you are? Think ya know everything …'

The Man in a Suitcase was sitting on a case with his back against another reading a Louis L'Amour novel. 'Anyone who doesn't know the answer to that has got to be arse …'

'Who rattled your cage?' asked Harry the Birdman.

Meanwhile, a large board had come in full of little nuggets that had to be taken into the wing and stowed.

'Here ya, get fuckin' round it,' shouted the hatch boss, Mr Magoo. 'Put the fuckin' books and twenty questions away and get stuck in … Let's have some red faces …'

'Fuckin' murderer,' someone muttered.

'Come on, stop fuckin' moanin', four men away.' So they all got stuck in and hooked the little heavy cases into the wing. After they had done that, they were horrified to see another board waiting for them.

'Fuckin' hell, those quay hands are keen, aren't they?' someone asked.

'Those cases are right by the shed door,' said The Birdman, so let's get rid of them as soon as possible then we can take it easy.' So for about an hour they sweated and cursed stowing the nuggets. One or two men had hooks, but the ones without found it a lot harder getting their fingers under them. Luckily, there was about an inch clearance, but it was still backbreaking work.

A docker's hook was a very handy tool, but most men did not possess one. I guarantee if there were eight men down below there would only be about two hooks between them. They did make things a lot easier, but you had to be very careful how you used them. A careless swing at a case and it might just bounce off. The end that curled like a letter C had a point on it, and unless you dug it into the case correctly this is what happened. Very handy for breaking wires on cases you wanted to plunder, or actually smashing the wood itself.

Some men were careless in the use of this tool and you had to watch your fingers when handling a case. They could be lost too when working down below; they might go clattering down the stringers right to the bottom. I've seen watches, combs, lighters, pipes, all dropped out of pockets by the lads when they are bending over or jumping from a case. All made nice presents for our friends at the destination. I have even seen false teeth go missing, and there is no chance of retrieving any of these articles unless you started discharging the cargo and that was never allowed.

You could use a hook on hessian bags, even paper bags, but you were not supposed to. For sacks you were issued with another lethal weapon called a scratcher. This was a short tool, similar to a hook but a shorter haft with a flat end studded with small sharp metal spikes. This didn't half hurt when it came into contact with your flesh ...

Both these tools, the hook and scratcher, had to be used carefully, because if you put your weight behind it and it came unstuck, you could go flying. You could be pulling a case over with your hook under the wire band and it suddenly snap. Happened to me once at Brock's yard. I had my hook around a wire, it snapped and I fell backwards into the low ground about six feet, but luckily I didn't hit any of the other cases. I hadn't been on the docks long at that time and I was shaken up by the experience, and although I threatened to leave this dangerous place of work, I stayed. I never stopped swearing for about thirty minutes; I suppose it was a sort of safety valve release.

Another use for the hook was for turning stubborn pins in shackles. A lot of men used to secrete a hook over their shoulder, either under or over the jacket, and some used their belts, placing the hook at the small of the back. I think you could get one made for about ten shillings back in the Sixties.

§

Sometimes they slipped up and sent in a case that contained something of interest, but not very often. When you saw a watchman down below, you had an idea there was something worth stealing. You could be in the lower hold working and the watchman would be in one of the tween decks watching you. He could see everything from up there; all he had to do was walk around and he could see the whole area down below. But most just sat down in one special place and never moved unless his boss came down to see what was happening. Or there could be whisky in the tween deck and the watchman was there just to keep his eye on that. But there were ways you could get at it if you were determined enough, and we always were. We always looked for the weakest link. I remember one such incident clearly. I was working with Jason B. down in the lower hold and the whisky was stowed above us in the lower tween. There was no chance of getting at it from there so we had a good look around. We were on the skin anyway and so had plenty of time to do so. I climbed up the stringers directly under the tween deck and had a close look at the deck-head and discovered there was a gap between the ship's side and the steel deck over my head. There was just enough to get a hand through but there was one problem. The gap had been filled in with concrete from above. But we never let little things like that put us off. Sometimes you could get it easily and other times we had to sweat. This was going to be sweating time. I had a go first, climbing up the wooden stringers and Jason passed me the steel bar. Hooking one leg inside the stringer just underneath the tween deck, I started attacking the concrete with the pointed end of the bar. Bits of concrete flew everywhere so I had to watch my eyes. After about half an hour Jason relieved me. Breaking the concrete made hardly any noise, unlike steel – that would have woken the dead. After about an hour I managed to get a hand through and touch the cardboard carton containing the bottles. So far so good. I always carried a knife for such a purpose. Still hooked over the stringer by one leg and holding on with one hand, I managed to cut the carton. I couldn't see it of course but that didn't matter. When I had managed to make a big enough hole, I had to use my fingers to get the first bottle out. There was just enough room to get it out completely. Once the first bottle was out the others were easier. All this had to be done with one hand. I felt like a magician pulling a rabbit out of a hat with that first bottle … where there's a will there's a way, as they say. Altogether we got about two dozen bottles from that almost inaccessible place. It was hard work but it was worth it. Poor Jason is no longer with us. I mean no disrespect but he would not have looked out of place on Devil's Island.

§

One thing about working on the docks – you were never bored. There was always something different happening. Different ships you were sent to, different types of cargo, different men in the opposite set or gang. Now and again you could be working with some Liverpool men. It was always exciting to me. Each day was a challenge. You never knew what was going to happen, up to a point, that is. If you were at a certain ship and loading a particular type of cargo, you had a fairly good idea of what was going on. But now and again something happened to change the routine. You might hear a whisper that whisky was coming in later, either down your hatch or someone else's. You could have a friend down the other hatch who perhaps put you on. Little things like that kept you going. To most of the men it was just a place of work and nothing else. They could have been working in a factory for all they cared. Not to me. The very fact of working on a ship was exciting enough.

I know a lot of men would disagree and say it's a load of shit. One ship was the same as any other. Enough said. Not to me. I thought each ship I worked on had a different character in some way – don't ask me what – I think the word intangible fits perfectly. You didn't spend eight hours down below unless you were too lazy to climb the ladder onto the deck. If for some reason you couldn't leave the ship (and that was only if the word came down that the timekeeper was going to make a check on the number of men working, or off the job), you had to hang around somehow. You could go to the mess room and play cards or talk. You could go and visit some of the other hatches and see what was going on. Take the piss out of your mates working down below while you were off. While you were there you could have a good look around and see what, if anything, was there to pinch. You could stay aboard if you didn't feel like going to the canteen, or outside the dock to one of the many small cafés, like the Sweat Box outside Vittoria Dock. You could always sunbathe if it was summer and the sun was out. We used to get up on the fo'c'sle head behind the windlass so the boss couldn't see us flaked out. Happy days at the Clan Line at Vittoria Dock or up at Lewis's Quay at Bidston.

One thing about staying aboard the ship sometimes was that if ever the timekeeper came round unexpectedly you weren't far away. But we never stayed aboard very often; there was always plenty to do elsewhere. You had time to go home (if you lived near enough) and do some decorating in the house. You could even go to the movies if you wanted to. In the summer we used to go to New Brighton baths and enjoy ourselves in the open air facilities. As I have said, there was no other job like the docks anywhere.

§

All hands were on the quay in the shed. There was a dispute at the China berth over men booking on and going straight out the gate. The Manager was a witness to all this and promptly sent the timekeeper aboard to get the numbers of the men working. The timekeeper was told to fuck off, as was the Manager. The men actually aboard the ship said they were not going to give their numbers in on the quay to the timekeeper and then again when they were actually working. The argument went on back and forth between the men and the Manager. The whole ship was at a standstill, and it looked like it could affect the other ships at the berth. Eventually, when all hands were in the shed refusing to give in to the management, he realised what could happen and was in a quandary. He didn't want to lose face, so he gave an order to all the men standing around. 'Right, you can get back to the Pen because you are not going to work on this ship ...'

Immediately, indignant voices were heard. 'Who the fuck does he think he is?'

'Who's not going aboard the fuckin' ship? Come on, lads, let's show him he's not messing us around.'

And they all trooped aboard again and started work. Wisely, the Manager lost himself quickly to fight another day.

Some men got drunk on the ship, and when the drink's in, the brain is definitely out ... so they feel confident and stash a few bottles around their waist and try and walk past the policeman on the gate. I don't know whether these men think they are invisible to the policemen when they have had a few drinks but drink does have some strange effects on them. Normally they would not dream of stealing from the cargo, and most times they got caught. They weren't regular thieves and it would be a one-off. I wish I could have collected a pound for every time I heard someone say, 'You will never get rid of those ...' I found a case full of women's panty girdles once at a Clan ship on the nights. And I heard this saying once again. But I sold the lot. The case was down below and to expedite matters I had the case taken out by crane. This saved a lot of ladder work carrying them all. From the quay it was a simple matter to transfer the lot to my car. If I make all this sound easy, believe me it was not. A lot of planning and thought had to go into it. And of course we all need that little bit of luck. You needed eyes in the back of your head to make sure no one was watching you. You mightn't be able to see someone across the dock who might have binoculars on you.

It was funny the day I was looking through my own I always carried and saw a certain policeman looking through his at me! But that's another story. It was just a matter of time before someone got their collar felt. You could go a long time being as careful as you could but sometimes the unexpected happened. But some of the lads were just plain stupid carrying off petty articles that were just not worth the risk. It wasn't worth losing your job for a few shillings but it did happen. All it took was a little common sense most times. For example, if you were on the ship, before you left you tried to make sure there was no danger on the quay. By this I mean you asked the lads had they seen anyone skulking around. Even if they said the coast was clear, by the time you got down the gangway and onto the quay the boys in blue could drive up in a van in a matter of seconds.

If this happened to you while you were carrying and you wanted to offload until the danger had passed, there were plenty of hiding places. But some would decide to brazen it out. I have been carrying through a shed and the police Land Rover following quietly. It was all down to nerve. Sure, the hairs on my neck would be standing out and I would be suppressing the terrific urge to run ... you could feel their eyes boring into your back. You would try to appear nonchalant and keep smiling.

§

We used to play football down an empty hatch. Sometimes when we were starting off at a ship with an empty hatch and were waiting for the cargo to come in, we would produce a ball and play shots in. Delay could occur when the quay or sheds were very congested or they couldn't get at the particular cargo needed. It happened sometimes. Any excuse for a lie-down on a handy case or bags. Or, for the more energetic, a game of football. Or, for the inquisitive type, a chance to go around and open a few cases. This could be done in several ways. Smash it open with a steel bar leaving it looking like a bomb had exploded. Or you could take your time and open it gently, have a look and then replace the wood looking unopened. The nails could even be knocked back in. The steel bands that used to bind the wood had to be broken of course and this could not be replaced, naturally. Walking around on top of the cargo could be very dangerous because of the numerous gaps that had to be left owing to the different shapes and sizes. Drums were the worst. Even with plenty of slabs down to give you a walking way. You could step on the end and it would be like stepping on the proverbial garden rake. There were many grazed and shinned legs working down below. You needed eyes in the back of your head most times. As I said, I had a fall at Brock's one time. The Whistling Kettle did the same once at the Clan. He fell off a high case and very nearly broke his spout. Mind you, he was lucky compared to what nearly happened to him later at another ship we were at. We were taking heavy iron railway wheels into the wings. These would come in on the hook, two or three at a time and would be landed against a wooden tub, with a slight lean in so they wouldn't fall over. You have to be very careful with these, as they could break your legs easily if they fell on you. You could take one into the wings if you were strong enough and kept the balance. But once it started to go, you had to leave it and get out of the way. Two men usually took one in and then went back to get another one. I was helping someone else, cannot remember his name, and Terry 'The Kettle' was standing by the tub. For some unknown reason he started to bring one in by himself. I heard him call my name frantically and we looked back to see him lying on the deck with a railway wheel across his lower legs. We feared the worst and ran to help him. After we had freed him we sent him out in a tub to go for a check-up just to be on the safe side. Poor Terry – despite his protestations we sent him to the first aid building on the quay. Then he told us why he didn't want to go. His feet weren't too clean and he had dirty socks on … we never laughed so much. But he was lucky that time; he only received a scraping on his legs. He had wanted to go home first to change his socks. Needless to say, he took some stick off us.

§

The Twelve Apostles. Twelve dockers were sitting in the mess room on a Blue Funnel ship at Vittoria Dock. The beer was flowing copiously, and all hands were very happy with all this free drink. There was much merrymaking and laughter. Larry B. was one of the merrymakers. The entrance of the police soon put the dampers on the proceedings. Hands that were holding glasses and cups and bottles disappeared like lightning into pockets and arms were folded. Faces became very serious as the police came in and pointed to the broached cargo. 'What's all this then?' they asked. Silence.

Eventually one docker ventured, 'What's all what?'

'This beer has been broached from the hatch. Who is responsible?'

Arms remained folded and hands stayed in pockets.

'Don't know nuttin' about da. We came in the mess room and this is how we found it. We wouldn't touch it, got nuttin' ta do with us.'

The police seemed determined to pin it on somebody. They asked another docker where the beer had come from.

'What beer?' he asked.

There were the usual threats but nothing could be proved. The remaining beer was confiscated and the party was over. Scenes like this were a common occurrence and unless you were caught in the act you nearly always got away with it. A man could be lying on the ground unconscious full of stolen whisky in his gut and nothing would happen to him, apart from being locked up for his own safety. The police would know he was full of stolen whisky but couldn't do anything about it. But if he had been found with a bottle stashed away somewhere, it would be a different story.

§

J.D. and I had hidden six tons of copper wire on the quay by placing some large case around it so it couldn't be seen. We were going to take it out on a lorry in the afternoon if all went well. But it didn't. After dinner, we looked for it and found it missing. Making a few discreet inquiries, we discovered that the ship's boss had found it and sent it into the hatch. Naturally we were choked. But undeterred we set about recovering it if we could. I went down No. 3 to have a look around and saw where it had been buried, but not too deep. Quickly we managed to get a crane driver willing to lift it out for a price. No. 3 is right under the bridge face and anyone with sharp eyes in one of the rooms could have seen the copper coming out instead of in. But everything went well and we managed to land it on a flat bed and off we went. But it was touch and go. There was a watchman on the deck at the time but as it wasn't the Poisoned Dwarf he didn't notice anything amiss. So we were quite pleased pulling it off.

§

There was a dispute going on at a Brock ship and when that happened the lads always made for the nearest pub to discuss the matter among themselves. Bobby C. and the Lip were sitting in the Park View talking about it when they were joined by a docker from another ship, M.M. Sitting at a nearby table was a railway worker and he asked M.M. what the trouble was. He replied, 'I don't fuckin' know but we ain't goin' back until we get it …'

§

T.O. was a hatch boss at an Anchor boat at the East Quay. In the tween decks there was an open stow of hundreds of cases of lager. The boss volunteered to distract the watchman's attention while they threw some cases down to the lads below. This was duly done and he was sorry later because as usual when something is free they drink like there is a severe drought on the way. Pretty soon all the lads slowed right down because of the intake of free lager and lost all interest in the job. Of course, all hell broke loose later; the watchman was sacked. Seldom Seen and Bobby C. were in the gang.

§

Once, Larry's Duck rescued an injured seagull from the dock. He took care of it and took it with him into the Red House pub and gave it rum. It was staggering about all over the place.

§

Billy M. was in bed after being on nights. His wife was out shopping. A burglar disturbed Billy, who grabbed him and worked him over good style. But he later got three months for using unnecessary force.

§

There was nothing more exciting than to go into an empty shed one morning and see nothing except a couple of stray cats skulking about, and then a huge articulated truck would come in loaded with whisky. Diesel fumes would fill the air and the hiss of air brakes and shouts. We would watch the proceedings for a few minutes on our way through to the next shed to the ship we were working on. Hungry eyes would watch the artic backing into the cage and a couple of stackers waiting to offload it. The head security man would be there talking to an old watchman. The next few days would see a marked difference. More and more vehicles would arrive and deposit their loads down on the deck all over the shed. The stow backs would be running around looking for wood to land the steel sheets on or even tractors, huge boxes with the tractors inside and the big wheels lying on the top of the case. Platers would be getting around with their little tins of blue paint and brush in hand marking the cases with their various designation marks. Karachi – Bombay – Port Louis – Port Said – Aden – Durban – Colombo – Hong Kong – Singapore – etc.

The cargo came in all shapes and sizes and different weights. Slowly the shed would fill up and more cranes and stackers would be called upon to handle the volume of traffic. It was like a beehive, and you had to be very careful because it became very hectic sometimes. A crane would come past at speed in reverse with the driver looking over his shoulder; one eye on the rear and the other eye on his load hanging on the hook. There was danger all around. All credit to these drivers doing a difficult job in a confined space. All this happened within a few days – from an empty shed to a hive of industry. If any of the wheeled vehicles don't get you, you can count on one of the many pigeons dropping its filthy load on you somewhere, and if you were fortunate enough to avoid all those, you would probably end up gassed with all the fumes that were emitted by the various vehicles. Look up to the roof of the shed and you would see clouds of poisonous fumes hanging over you like a nuclear fallout, so you couldn't win anyway. Even when you went out of the shed and onto the quay where the ships tied up, you had to watch your step. Same thing happened here too. Only this time you had to watch the dockside cranes that ran up and down the quay on wheels fixed to rails. There wasn't much chance of getting hit by one of these, but when they lifted cargo up in the air it was a different matter. They had no control over a pallet board full of drums which could fall off from a great height. The danger was incredible.

§

When working down below with just four men sometimes the boss would send the timekeeper around to see how many men were missing from the jog. This always caused problems. Most times he would look over the coaming and shout out. 'Sing out your numbers lads …' Sometimes the men absent would leave their numbers just in case something like this happened. But there was not much you could do if the timekeeper wanted to see all eight men. But you always tried to bluff him. So four men would sing out their numbers and then do the same with the other numbers. If the timekeeper was satisfied, all good and well, but if he wanted a show of heads, too bad. But you could still try and bluff him by putting on someone else's hat or coat and letting the timekeeper see you and hope for the best. Sometimes the lads would get awkward and tell him to come down the hatch and see for himself. This would enrage him all the more and didn't do any good because I never ever saw a timekeeper come down to check all the men. He would mark the other four men absent and report it. The guilty men would then have to go on the carpet and get their knuckles rapped slightly and warned about their future behaviour. Plus they would lose some money. But this happened quite often and no one was ever sacked. But it all went down on your record.

Most of the timekeepers were OK but a couple were snides. I was only ever cleared out once and that was because the other men we relied on let us down and there is nothing you can do about it, except give the same men a very wide berth next time. These same men just wanted to have their cake and eat it.

I will never forget the timekeeper over in Liverpool who came over the hatch and shouted down to a Liverpool docker we were working with to go home immediately as a member of his family was seriously ill. Later on we were told it was a regular thing with this man. I think it was the Electric Mouse (should have been rat) had this arrangement with the timekeeper who was a friend to do this to get him off and into his favourite boozer. The lengths some people will go to just to go boozing with his cronies. I remember that ship very well because Danny Kaye and I got some tins of fabulous curry powder from it. Great stuff. It lasted a long while. That was the only good thing about it really.

In the Sixties we only had to book on at 8 a.m. and that was it. But shortly afterwards they brought in the new system of making everyone report back for work at 1 p.m. as well, which didn't go down very well with the lads. But there was nothing anyone could do about it.

§

'Who's got a hook to lend me?' asks someone.

'Where's your own?'

'Lost it down the stringers at Bibby's.'

'When was that?'

'About six months ago …'

'Some fuckin' Paki's got that now. He'll be made up.'

'Get your fingers under this case anyway and lets get it stowed before it takes root … four men away, you know. Come on, red faces, all together … that's it. Smashin'. Put the sling under it so we can turn it. Come on, once over and right in its place. Who's not fuckin' liftin'?'

'Hang on. Me fuckin' lighter's fell …'

'Jesus Christ! Not again. Why don't you put it somewhere safe where it can't fall out?'

'Got to gerrit back. She bought it for me birthday. There'll be murder if I don't get it.'

'Can you see it?'

'No. But if we heave this case out we might see it.'

'No chance. It's probably gone all the way to the bottom.'

'Get the fuckin' dogs and we'll try and get that case out. If we can't see it you've had it, OK?'

'Fair enough, but we gotta try.' Someone brought over the dogs.

'Hold yours steady while he takes the weight,' signalling to the deckhand.

The steel dogs bit into the wood and it lifted slowly out of its place, and there was the lighter on top of the case under it.

'You stuffy bastard, if you fell down the shithouse pan you'd come up with a gold watch ... let's get this fuckin' case back in before they start screamin' about the job stoppin' ... pass the word will ya ...'

The sound of splintering wood was heard over in the corner of the hatch. They looked over and saw the Fugitive breaking into a case with the bar.

'Wastin' your time there. There's fuck all in that.'

'Well, just let me find out for sure, OK? You never know.'

The sound of splintering wood reverberated all over the hatch. Anxious faces looked up to the main deck and tween decks in case someone was watching.

'Keep the fuckin' noise down will ya? Sounds like you're ripping the bowels out of the ship ...'

§

Himmler and a few friends had to four hook Cowboy out the gate one day because he was legless. Between them they managed to carry him out past the policeman on the gate. They stood him up and asked him how he felt. Cowboy stood against the wall and said, 'I feel great now lads, thanks. Before you go, have a drink on me.' And brought out a bottle of whisky they didn't even know he had ...

§

A Wallasey man working with a Liverpool man on the Golden Mile made a rash statement to the latter: 'If you are ever over this side, please feel free to call in, any time you feel like, OK?'

T.B. regretted asking the man later. Sunday morning he was lying in bed with his wife enjoying a sleep in when there was a very loud knocking at the front door. It was 8 a.m. and he wondered who it was. Turned out it was Jerry the Lion with his wife and kids. He made them welcome and gave them breakfast. Then dinner. They made no move to go. Stayed for tea. Still no sign they were leaving. The evening dragged on slowly. T.B. thought they might be staying for supper so he got into his pyjamas and started winding the clock. It was then they decided to go.

§

I was down below at the Anchor at the East Quay when I was still fairly new and didn't know everyone yet. But I did know about a certain Peeping Tom who was a deckhand. The discussion got around to perverts and I was going on about what I would do to one. I felt someone kicking me but of course I didn't think anything of it. I mentioned this Peeper's name and what a so and so he was and should be hanged. You can imagine how I felt when I was told his father was in the opposite gang and he heard every word I said.

I felt ashamed of myself for embarrassing the man like that. He was very good about it though. He explained a few things to me. I apologised for my outburst; it was the least I could do in the circumstances. We became good friends. But it just goes to show you never know who is listening when you slag someone.

§

Deaf Billy was on nights at the Clan. Women's wool cardigans were available and all hands were helping themselves. Billy helped himself and came off the ship to go home. He only lived nearby but on a sudden impulse he decided to go to the toilet before he did so.

While in there he stripped all the cardigans off and put them on the floor. Then he decided to put the cardigans over his shoulders instead of around his waist, which was the common practice. Then he started walking up Gorsey Lane and was part of the way up when a police Land Rover pulled up alongside him and two policemen jumped out and demanded to search him. Billy was sweating as they patted him down but for some reason they never checked his shoulders. They never discovered the cardigans and Billy got away with it. They were still in the cellophane wrappers. If he had not gone to the toilet that would have been it.

§

Took a whole consignment of electric irons once from the shed at the Clan. They were on a pallet board inside the fine goods area and guarded by a watchman, but it was fairly easy to distract him for a few minutes. It takes just as long to get the forks of a stacker under them and get away. I took the lot out in the boot of my Mini. Takes longer but sometimes you cannot get a van on short notice.

Did the same once with a consignment of typewriters but we put them back because the numbers and letters were in Pakistani. This sometimes happens and you have to be careful what you take. You have to be certain the commodity you take is compatible to this country. Even the electical goods because the voltage could be different in the country where it is bound for.

Big Bobby W. took a load of sewing machines out but couldn't get rid of them because they were the wrong voltage. They had been destined for Bombay.

§

J.D. and I had our eyes on a hundred brand-new tyres in a City Line shed on the Golden Mile, from Duke Street bridge right up to Lewis's Quay. We had a van laid on to come and pick them all up in the afternoon. Went for our dinner looking forward to a nice little earner later. But a certain pipe-smoking checker had beaten us to it. All's fair in love and war, they say.

§

J.D. and I were on the quay as usual. There was nothing going. The shed was just starting to fill up. So we were quite content to coast along until something happened. And it did. But not in the way we expected. A lorry came into the shed piled high with all sorts of drink. Whisky, brandy, gin and all sorts of wines. We got the info from a friend in the know that the driver never even had consignment notes. Believe it or not the driver had no idea what he had on the lorry. He had picked it up in Liverpool with its load and knew the name of the ship at least. While they were making phone calls to the people concerned we got busy. As the load couldn't be checked against consignment notes it was fair game. The driver had gone off somewhere; he must have thought once the load was in the shed it was safe. Nothing could have been further from the truth. The vultures were waiting to pick the carcass. There were even cases of champagne, but we weren't interested in that garbage – we wanted the whisky. We managed to get about a dozen cases before we had to scatter because the prick of a checker was seen hurrying back. He must have realised what would happen, but he was too late.

§

Billy C. (Chivvy) was the boss at Smith's. A very fast walker. He was seen by men going to work who were in a car. This was on the four bridges. They offered him a lift. He refused as he was in a hurry.

§

While T.R. (Talking Horse) was working at the Bidston Dock on the mini shift, on the quay were parked a couple of fire engines of the Land Rover type. Equipped with aluminium ladders of the extending type. During the evening he stripped one of the fire engines of its ladders and put them on top of his own car and drove out the gate with them.

Another time he stripped a chopper bike to pieces and took it out under the bonnet of his car. This was on nights in Liverpool. He also took out twelve electric kettles the same way. The funniest time was when he took out thousands of packets of Durex from a Chilean ship at the Bidston. He was on nights at the Clan with L.R., another crane driver. They saw a big chest in one of the old offices they used to have; it had four iron wheels and could be towed anywhere. It was put in a corner of the shed and left. So they got curious and opened it. They thought they had cracked it. Inside were bangles, rings, and assorted pieces of jewellery. But they found out it was all cheap and nasty trash. Probably going to some Indian bazaar. T.R. had six kids and as each one was born so he would take out a few hundredweight of tinned milk just to make sure they had plenty.

§

J.D. and I were on the mini shift at a City boat one evening at the North Quay. We managed to get two sackfuls of alarm clocks up onto the deck out of the hatch. I was standing on the quay waiting for him to pass them to me so I could hide them somewhere until I was ready to take them in my car. I had one on my back and I felt like Father Christmas when suddenly the ship's boss came around the corner and saw me. I fully expected the worst but all he said was 'Get lost – fast … and I did.'

§

Petrol bogie was being driven at the China berth at Vittoria Street. The driver misjudged the edge of the quay and went into the dock. The save-all that is placed against the ship's side nearly saved him, but it wasn't secured enough, so in he went like a ton of bricks.

There was a loud splash as he did so and the bogie went down to the bottom. He surfaced spluttering and was promptly asked by a comedian standing on the quay, 'Did you switch the engine off?' Everyone fell about but the swimmer wasn't amused. Understandable.

§

On nights at the Bidston Dock at a Harrison boat, down No. 2 and we had everything going. Shoes, shirts, tools of every description, including Stanley planes, ratchet-type screwdrivers, hammers, drills, saws, etc. It was about three in the morning and raining cats and dogs. The gate was very dangerous and the odds were stacked against getting out in the morning without getting pulled. So we decided to fill some sacks and make our way across the Bidston tip, which in itself was very dangerous on account of the pitfalls all over the place. Les and I were making such a trip across to stash our loot near some houses to be picked up later when we finished work at 7 a.m. I remember carrying those sacks on my back with all the hard edges digging into my flesh. At one point Les asked me to look down near my feet and I did so. There were about ten large rats scurrying about; they were too fat to move quickly. All sorts of rubbish was dumped there including foodstuffs, so they were well fed. Nevertheless, that didn't stop us. We dumped everything near a wall and went back to the ship across the Bidston moss and back onto the quay where all the cargo was stowed. We saw the ship's boss coming towards us so we hid behind one of the cases. By rights we should have still been working on the ship. Anyway he saw us flattened out trying to hide. But he just looked at us strangely and we just walked away without saying a word.

§

You could be down below and there might only be two or three hooks in use out of eight. Not every docker carried one. They were definitely very useful for turning cases over and getting them in position when stowing them. If they were heavy cases and had to be moved into the wings, your hook saved you a lot of hard work and maybe saved your fingers from getting hurt. A simple rope sling could help you get your case far away too. Just lay it down in an untidy heap, drop the case on it and you could turn it any way you wanted it. Or a simple block of wood would do the same job. Or you could use the steel bar. There was a hard way to do things and an easy way. But most times it was pure physical strength that did it. Nothing worse than to drop a case in position and see it fall awkward and jam. So it had to come out or be manoeuvred with your hook or the bar. At least you could always get a wire around it and heave it out and try again. But you never let little setbacks like this upset you. Of course, we used to take the piss out of whoever it happened to. Say things like 'You couldn't stow shite in a bucket' or 'Who hired you, Walt Disney?' Some of the lads didn't want to know about being the stevedore, or have the bar as it was known. Couldn't take the hassle of a hatch boss snarling at them or the so-called responsibility. We all got stuck in really and helped each other. The cargo came in all shapes and sizes, some heavy, some light, and some very heavy. I have known little cases weigh up to three hundredweight; you wouldn't believe it sometimes. You would get a little case that was a little ballbreaker and one that was six times as big and you could turn it over by yourself. Same with drums. Some you could head up, 40-gallon size, and others like Arsenite would make you sweat.

When you had to hit the deck-head – that is, go as high as you could – you had to use the step system to stow the drums. There were various ways you could do this: use the step system or have a couple of wooden tubs and use landing boards. These were dangerous and could be mistaken for springboards sometimes. But there was no other way to stow stuff. You really had to improvise a lot and use your imagination to get cargo in inaccessible parts of the hatch. Heaving in large, heavy cases was a problem sometimes. There might not be anywhere to fasten your block so you had to use a piece of iron weighing about thirty pounds called a 'Bulldog', which was supposed to clamp onto a part of the ship called beams – actually the thing was called a Scotch BeamDog. It was a helluva job trying to get this infernal thing in place, especially if it had to be fixed away from the ship's side. Lots of straining and red faces. If it dropped on your head, it would have killed you stone dead.

§

Flags of all nations could be seen in the docks and at anchor in the river. Panama, Liberia, Costa Rica, Greece, Italy, Cyprus, India, United States, Brazil, Finland, Poland and many, many more. Ships of all shapes and sizes. From modern-day liners to old tramp steamers like the Second World War vintage Forts, Parks, Empires, Victory, and the most famous of all steamer, the Liberty or Sams as some people knew them. The biggest fleet of one particular type of ship ever built, nearly three thousand built in the US during the war. I have seen three in the Huskisson Dock at one time, and three in the Canada. I suppose during the war there were many more than that. The 1950s and '60s were the heyday to my knowledge for shipping on a grand scale but just after 1970 it had thinned out considerably. We started signing on a lot because there was no work. I suppose the writing was already on the wall. I had heard some rumours a lot earlier but I didn't really think it would come off. But it sure did.

§

I was about to go out in my car one day with some stuff stashed away in a secret compartment. Half a dozen bottles of whisky and some toothpaste. Bitter Belly asked me for a lift as I was going his way, but I explained to him I was carrying and we might get a pull. He wasn't bothered, as he was clean. So off we went. I was approaching Duke Street entrance ready to get off the dock estate when Farmer's Boy materialised out of the slight drizzle. I didn't even know he was in hiding behind all those big cases on the quay. He stood in front of my car with his arms outstretched. We just stared at each other for a few seconds. I watched his face through the windscreen wipers. I got the impression he thought I would take off as soon as he moved. Eventually he walked round to my window and he gestured to me to wind my window down. I did so and asked him what he wanted, although it was fairly obvious. He asked me to step out while he searched. Billy got out as well and he searched him and then Billy started walking. I told him I would pick him up in a few minutes.

I sincerely thought so, because, even if the Farmer found something, there was no way I would have accepted it meekly. I would have taken off. He searched me thoroughly and then turned his attention on the car. First the boot, then under the bonnet. Inside the car as well. He found nothing, although his hand was practically on the loot. I got back in the car and said to him, 'Alright now, Bob? Satisfied? Can I go?' He looked at me with displeasure and asked me to get out again. I got out again and stood by the car complaining he was making me late for dinner.

My stomach was starting to knot by now and I was considering what action to take. He seemed determined to find something in the car. Maybe I shouldn't have asked what he was looking for the first time and he might have let me go. He looked under the bonnet again and in the boot. He even got on his knees to look under the car. Then he started on the inside again, looking in the pockets in the rear. Under the rear seat cushions. The whisky was directly under the seat. By this time I was getting impatient and started nagging him. Anything to distract him from what he was doing. Finally, he gave up and grudgingly allowed me to go. He didn't know how close he came to being pushed to the ground. The beauty of the job was that you had to be caught red-handed with stolen property. Now, if I had thrown him to the ground and got away, I knew that later I would have been arrested. But my excuse would have been that I was approached by this man who looked as if he was about to attack me so I retaliated and got away. I would have pleaded ignorance of him being a policeman. Probably I would have been fined but the point is that I would not have lost my job. That was the most important thing. A similar incident had happened to me a few years earlier which will prove my point, but more about that later.

I still carried on taking stuff out the rest of the week and nothing happened. It's like I said, it is just like Russian roulette – you never know when a policeman is going to jump out of hiding and stop you. Mind you, it wasn't a matter of life or death; the most you lost was your job.

§

Tommy offered a friend a lift and told him to wait in his car. His friend did so. Tommy got in and drove to the gate. He was stopped by the police and searched. His friend had half a dozen tins of Milo hidden under his seat unknown to Fat T. Luckily, his friend swore the driver didn't have any idea what he had done and was believed by the police. The Milo Kind was done for it and was fired soon afterwards.

§

Rubber Gob, a deckhand at the time, was on nights at the Clan. This particular night he was on a winch at No. 3 hatch. These winches were a few feet away from the bridge face and he was driving one of these. All through the night he was offered a break but refused. Everyone was amazed at his conscientiousness. It was much later they found out the reason why. Directly behind him were the windows to the saloon and some cabins. It was in one of these rooms one of the ship's officers and his wife (or girlfriend) were engaged in a lot of sexual activity all through the night. He had been watching his own private blue movie and didn't want to lose a moment, except when he had to get some cargo in.

A lot of this peeping went on when there were women aboard, whether they be officers' wives or prostitutes. I heard of one man, Porthole Pete, who was actually seen hanging by his feet from the boat deck looking into one porthole. Another man had to be prised from one alleyway porthole bodily as there was a queue waiting to have a look at what was going on.

§

Not long after I started on the docks, maybe a couple of years, I very nearly lost my book for good. It all happened because I did not listen to good advice at the time. I was on nights at a Clan ship at the old Wharf. By this time I was having a go at carrying off. We had opened some tea chests and found them to be full of ornaments, the type that you fix to the wall. Small figures made of plaster in the shape of characters such as a pirate's head or an Indian chief with full headdress. I and another chap I was working with decided to help ourselves. We finished our welt at 6 a.m. and decided to go then against the advice of some others who recommended it would be far safer to go off later with the rest of the men. Safety in numbers. We didn't fancy hanging around till then and off we went. I had a Lambretta scooter at that time, and I gave this other chap a lift to the bus stop outside the dock gate. That was the idea anyway. He had a bag full of these ornaments and I had a bag full and some inside my clothes. It was daylight and there wasn't a soul around as we cruised up the avenue between the two sheds. We turned the corner and saw the policeman on duty at the gate directing traffic. There was no one else in sight. It was my intention to go past this policeman without stopping even if he had asked me to. But just as we were approaching him, around the corner came a police Land Rover which stopped directly in front of me, and two policemen jumped out and signalled for me to stop. My friend begged me not to stop, but I had no intention anyway. The policeman had his arm out and I actually touched it as I carried on past him heading for the gate. The other policeman on point duty signalled for us to stop as well, but I just ignored him and carried on. I couldn't go fast because of the weight, but I knew I just couldn't accept defeat. There were traffic lights ahead on red but I couldn't wait, naturally, so I went through. I was trying to think where I could possibly hide just so we could get rid of the evidence. I heard the Land Rover coming up behind. There was a garage just across the road out of sight of my pursuers, with a low brick wall just in front of the pumps. Of course, it was closed at that time in the morning. The wall was just high enough to hide us if we flattened out. My friend was standing there like a lemon, and I had to drag him down with me, telling him it was our only chance. I remember I felt foolish doing it, because I fully expected the Land Rover to pull in and one of them to come out with a sarcastic remark. As we lay there behind this low wall (it was only about eighteen inches high), we heard the engine of the Land Rover close by as they turned the corner. This would put them directly opposite where we were lying on the floor behind the wall. I could smell the petrol from my scooter, which was lying on its side, and my arm was across my friend's body because he was panic-stricken. I told him to be quiet and wait. Slowly, the Land Rover kept going down the street, and when I thought it was safe, I stood up and had a quick peep and saw them about two hundred yards away going away, but they were looking for us. Quickly, I stood my scooter up and got rid of all my stuff. He did the same, and then took off for the bus stop. At first, the scooter wouldn't start, as it was flooded. But finally it got going and off I went heading up the street. I felt happy because I had nothing on me, but I had a feeling I would be overtaken soon. I was. About a mile up the road they stopped me and were they mad. I was threatened and jostled, but I did not retaliate in any way. Accusations flew thick and fast, but I denied everything. Against my will, they made me leave my scooter where it was while I was put in the back of the Land Rover. I protested strongly about the possibility of some thief taking my scooter, but they didn't want to know. We made our way back to the garage where they discovered the loot. Smiles all round except from me. They put all the stuff in the back and went back to the ship. From there to the police station on the dock estate and more questions. The CID man they called wasn't too pleased at that hour in the morning to interview me. I said nothing except that I was innocent. He was nice enough. What about not stopping for three policemen? And going through a red light? he asked. He had a point there. I just pleaded tiredness coming off the nights and wanted to get home and get my head down. He told me my house was being searched and actually apologised, but I knew this would happen. After a few hours, I was released; I didn't get completely away with it. I was fined £10. Five for not stopping for the policemen and five for going through a red light. But I didn't lose my job. I could have made it easier for them and come clean, because that is what they expected. But if you keep your mouth shut you're better off. But it didn't do me any good a few years later when I was eventually caught and sent down. The other chap involved and myself had a good laugh the following night. Needless to say, I never touched anything else while I was at that ship. But I was pulled a few times anyway. Once they know you're a bagman, you can expect it. They even had at that time all the licence plate numbers of all the thieves typed down at various points. Just like we knew the numbers of all the unmarked police vehicles.

Eleven o'clock that night, I reported for work as usual and nothing was said and no action was taken. What could they do?

I knew I was on their hit list from the time of the scooter incident. They were very annoyed when I refused to stop for them coming off the dock estate loaded. That was close. But not as close as at a City boat on the Golden Mile. We borrowed a small van to take some stuff away. It's no secret how it's done. A friend lends you the van, and if anything goes wrong, you ring him up right away and he tells the police it's been stolen. Everybody knows different, but try and prove it. We had done one trip with this van, taking over £2,000 worth of tools, planes, ratchet-type screw-drivers, drills, wood chisels, stuff like that. We got this away easily and came back again to get some more. This time we were taking cloth, dressing gowns, shirts, ties, etc., all in wooden cases. I parked the van in the avenue outside the dock shed near the door. This is where I nearly got captured red-handed through the stupidity of one man. We had posted the necessary lookouts while we loaded the van. I was actually inside the van distributing the load evenly over the deck. J.D. was standing near the front off side and I could see him. Suddenly, he tells me to get down and stay in the van as the police van had sneaked out of the shed right at the rear of our van. I was caught inside. I couldn't get out because they would see me and know right away I was up to no good. I risked a glance through the rear window and saw the blue police van almost stopped. J.D. told me not to move until he said so. So I had to crouch down and watch J.D.'s face. He told me they were looking at him and were undecided what to do. Finally, he told me to get out quickly as the van had moved, and I would not be seen getting out. I was out in a flash. They knew something was going on, I think, but weren't too sure what. We watched them leave slowly and park up further down the dock road about five hundred yards away. I was all for driving the van away, but J.D. said it wasn't worth it. I hated to lose the goods after all the hard work. I got my binoculars and had a good look at the police van. It was funny to see one of them looking straight back at me through his binoculars! I had to laugh. They were definitely waiting for the van to move, so we decided to ring the owner quickly. Only just in time too. The next minute the police arrived from all directions and blocked our van in. By this time, J.D. and I were standing on the deck of the City boat watching the proceedings. You would have thought they were after bank robbers ...

Well, that was one round we lost. Not bad – one out of two. If looks could have killed, we would have died. They nearly had yours truly that time. The reason was because one man we posted as lookout fell down on the job. The police van had come along the quay from Duke Street and sneaked in the shed and came out in the avenue. If they had come a few minutes earlier, they would have seen us throwing the cases in the back of our van. There were that many ways we had to watch, but you cannot guarantee anything. We were lucky that day. It was at the same ship we got something out of the shed; I think it was a three-hundredweight case. The little old watchman was using the case as a chair, and it seemed as if he were nailed to it; he just wouldn't move. We tried all sorts. In the end, J.D. got on a stacker and forced him to move by manoeuvring it in such a way the man's life was in danger. It worked anyway. He went somewhere else. We had our van on the quay in between the ship and the shed. All hands could see it. But we had no choice. We couldn't afford to hang around long, so J.D. had to get the case out of the shed and bring it out and put it in the van all in one fluid movement. Which he did. There was about an inch either side, but he managed it. Unfortunately, the watchman came out and saw us shutting the doors of the van and knew we were up to no good and went to blow us up. But he was too late anyway. You just can't go up to someone and accuse them of stealing something that isn't there. It's just not done. Different if you are caught red-handed, and even then you don't admit it. Why make it easy for them? To us it was all a big laugh anyway. If there was something we needed a crane or a stacker for, we would ask some of the lads who liked to dabble. If no one was available, we would do it ourselves if we could. Some men nearly had a coronary when you asked them to do something. We always offered payment for services rendered.

I always admired these crane drivers, the way they worked in such restricted areas. They had to contend with the cargo everywhere. In some of the old sheds like Brock's they had low beams running fore and aft, and steel posts everywhere as well. Sometimes they had to lower their jib and literally drag the cargo along the shed floor under these beams until they found a place where there was more room overhead. They had to be something of a contortionist to drive those awkward cranes, and they didn't have power-assisted steering either. Not only did they have to watch out for the cargo stacked everywhere, the poor old docker was fair game. You needed eyes in the back of your head at all times.

§

In the Fifties you could see the Cunarders such as the *Carinthia, Saxonia, Franconia, Ivernia, Media, Parthia* and maybe their smaller ones that used to run to the Mediterranean, the *Brescia, Bantria.* Elder Demsters – *Apapa, Accra, Aureol, Onitsha* and many more. The *Arakaka, Arafura, Ebani, Eboe, Raphael, Sacremento, Sarmiento,*

Cuzco, Kypros, Tabor, Rippingham Grange, Malmesbury, Cheshire, Devonshire and the *Beaverdell, Beaverglen, Beaverlake*. If these ships weren't alongside you would see them in the river waiting to go in. All sorts of tankers would be coming and going to and from the Persian Gulf or the West Indies. Texaco, Shell, Eagle Oil, BTC (British Tanker Corporation), Blue Star, Clan Line, Federal, Bookers, Manchester Liners, Union Castle, Shaw Savill. All these and many more were to be seen in dock in Liverpool and Birkenhead. Greek, Panama, Cyprus, Singapore, Liberia and others with a flag of convenience flying would be seen. All the above have long gone now to various breakers' yards in Hong Kong, Formosa (Taiwan), Spain. Most were never seen again unless one crept back in with a new name and foreign flag. At the time of writing, Birkenhead docks looks like a ghost town. The once-busy quays are deserted now and the compound where they used to store all the export cars is bare. Grass is growing everywhere, the sheds are empty and all sorts of plants are growing in the gutters high above. The only ships that come in here now are those that are to be laid up for a while or are awaiting resale to some Greek in Piraeus. Those quays used to be very congested with cases and hundreds of oil drums all stacked over ten feet high, all securely wedged and maybe a heavy case at either end to make sure they didn't roll away. The seagulls can sit around with the pigeons now for hours without being disturbed by ships blowing off steam or air brakes being applied or shunting trains. The Clan Ghost can never again leap out from behind a case and scare the pants off an unsuspecting docker or a woman visiting a ship to sell her favours, and this did happen in fact. As an afterthought, maybe he didn't have to in her case. Of course, there are many shipping lines I haven't mentioned because the list is endless. But the older dockers will remember them all even before the Fifties. That is when I became aware of the volume of shipping that called here. I could have mentioned the CPR or Monks – with all their little coasters – Savage, Everards, Borchard, Bowater, Strick, Guinea Gulf, Head Line. I could go on and on. They will never be seen again, I don't think. I am only glad I did see most of these wonderful ships and a lot more. *Jason, Ajax, Cyclops, Tantalus, Mentor, Hector, Stentor, Charon* – all fabulous names from Greek mythology and all Blue Funnel ships that graced the quays at Birkenhead docks, and Liverpool. Vittoria Dock used to hold three at a time. Before my time on the docks there used to be one called the *Tyndareus* which was unique I believe in that she had nine hatches. Unless you are really interested in mythology, you would never know that Tyndareus was the husband of Leda and the father of Helena. It was one of the first books I ever read as a child, the *Iliad*. But I know a lot of men only wanted to know what the ship was paying and if there was anything for the bag or if there were any nights going. I remember one man who couldn't tell you where he was once down the hatch. You would be down No. 2, lower tween on the port side. He wouldn't have a clue. And I don't suppose it mattered really. *Maidan, Magdapur, Mahout, Masirah* – all place names in India. Belonging to another famous line, Brocklebank. Used to run to Chittagong, Calcutta, Colombo, Port Said, Seychelles, even the Gulf ports of the USA – New Orleans, Mobile, Houston. In the Sixties they had one of the old Fort type built in Canada, the *Mahsud*, still steaming. Not forgetting the one that took a direct hit during the war, the *Malakand* blew up causing a lot of damage. Anchor Donaldson used to run from the East Quay to Egypt, India, Pakistan and the USA. Never cared much for that berth, too near the police station just across the road from the shed.

Regular callers to Birkenhead were the *Indian Pioneer, Trader, Merchant Endeavour*, mainly Victory types built in the USA, 1945, all electric winches, steam turbines that could push her along at a steady fourteen knots. All been long scrapped by now. Owned by Indian Steamships & Co.

The Clan Line ships were all named after Scottish clans. *Clan Irvine, Fraser, Donaldson*, etc. A lot of these were refrigerated ships running to Durban, East London, Beira, Lourenço Marques, Walvis Bay, Capetown and many other places on the African continent.

T&J Harrison's with their distinctive funnel markings, two of fat and one of lean. *Astronomer, Arbitrator, Herdsman, Linguist, Scholar, Historian, Colonial, Planter, Specialist*. Unmistakable names. India and Ceylon, and from Liverpool to the West Indies, Trinidad, Barbados, Jamaica, St Kitts, Antigua, Montserrat, Dominica and the Gulf ports of the USA – Mobile, New Orleans, Houston.

§

You had to laugh at some of the antics grown men would get up down below. Very ingenious some of the moves they made to get at the booze. I have seen them use a long, flexible plastic pipe to siphon the stuff from many feet below, from steel kegs that have been buried under tons of cargo, And the men who tried to look slimmer than they were despite having about six yards of cloth wrapped around their middle. 'How do I look?' they would ask their mates, apprehensively. The game was to take your clothes right off and then wrap the stuff around your body and then try and put your clothes back on. Some men took more than was wise sometimes, but this was taking a chance. If it was in the summer all the more hazardous because you looked suspicious wearing too many clothes. I have taken my share of topic, mohair, worsted, wool, etc. I never really liked taking the stuff but you could always sell it.

While on the subject of cloth, I can recall a very amusing incident that happened at a Clan ship at Lewis's Quay, Bidston. In the gang was a Nigerian chap, Izzy B., with a reputation of being a very good boxer a few years ago. I had the pleasure of working with Izzy many times. He had put on a few pounds around the middle but he was no marshmallow. This chap wasn't a bag man but this time he thought he would take some of the cloth we had going. We tried to dissuade him of course, but he was determined. So we helped him get dressed. He took more than he should have really. We helped him put his clothes back on with great difficulty and he was perspiring a lot by the time we had finished. I think he had about eight yards in all. He looked twice as big now. But we told him he looked good. He kept asking me, 'How do I look, Lenny?' I reassured him he looked OK. The Leper and Les T. looked on. We were just knocking off and were preparing to get up on deck. This is where Les and his dry sense of humour nearly caused our friend to have a heart attack. He was assured there was no one in sight on the quay and it was all clear. But just as he was stepping out of the trunkway onto the deck, Les told him that Lloydy and the Farmer's Boy were coming aboard the ship … the shock to that man's system was terrible. He had been in the ring with some hard men and never even blinked, but it was a different kind of courage needed to walk past a policeman with stolen property on you. I thought it was cruel really what Les had done. But we got him off the ship OK. I could have sworn he had gone almost white with fear for a short while. But that's the way it was down there; you had to have a great sense of humour although it was sorely tried at times. We gave Izzy the biggest fright of his life down below one time. He was down a hole and we asked the deckhand to lower away on top of him. He was never frightened in the ring but he was terrified when he saw that ton case coming down on top of him. I hope he has forgiven us for that little caper.

When you went to have your cloth made into a suit you had to choose your tailor very carefully. But you can slip up. I went with some friends to a well-known tailor in Birkenhead, very well known, with a small bolt of worsted to get made up. I asked the tailor to make me a couple of suits out of my own material. 'Sure,' he said. He unrolled my bolt of worsted onto his bench. I could have died when it opened up disclosing the little Union Jack motifs indicating it was for export only. But the tailor didn't even blink. 'Nice bit of cloth this,' was all he said. I felt uneasy in case he thought twice about it and blew us up. but he never did. After all, we were good customers of his and business is business.

I remember once on a City boat on the Golden Mile (Wallasey) we got some fine cloth from down below and tried to sell it to the Indian crew members. We went aft with it and tried bargaining with them but they wanted it for next to nothing. We tried to coax them but they wouldn't have it. We couldn't take it back to the hatch and we didn't want to give it to them for nothing so out of spite I threw it over the side into the dock. I realised right away I had done a stupid thing as it would float for a while and some nosy parker on the quay might spot it and realise what was going on. But nothing happened. But I was determined the Indians were not going to get it for nothing. You had to be very careful when dealing with crew members because they would snitch on you to the Mate, yet they were the biggest thieves.

§

J.D. and I managed to get a few tons of brass from inside a cage on the quay once at the China. There was a watchman inside too. But he seemed to be glued to the one spot all the time so we thought we might have a chance if he stayed there. We borrowed a crane – J.D. was driving it and I got inside the cage without being seen and put some wires around the brass, and J.D. lifted it out. We didn't know if the watchman would suddenly decide to take a walk around and spot us so we were sweating for a few minutes. But he stayed exactly where he was all the time. It took us about ten minutes to get it out and then we used a stacker to get it away from that area to a safe place down the shed. We had a truck coming to pick it up after dinner. Our troubles weren't over by any means. The truck arrived and we parked him in between the two huge sheds. You can put lookouts all over the place but there is always a loophole. Our driver had no nerves anyway. Just as we were putting the last pallet board on the flat deck a policeman appeared from nowhere and walked across the avenue about two hundred yards away. Even if he had looked our way it might have looked innocent enough – two men loading a vehicle. It did happen now and again a vehicle would come into the dock and pick up something that couldn't be taken on a particular ship or had been turned back by the customs for some reason.

§

There was a young docker who, strangely enough, was never down below. He was always working on the quay. Usually the younger men worked down below, but not always; there were quite a lot of older men among them. If you were not quite as fit as the younger men, or had some sort of disability, you could perhaps get a lighter job on the quay. But you could also get a backbreaker on the quay. There was no reason this man should have been on the quay all the time. He seemed a fit person. But then he died suddenly. Some of the lads went to his funeral to pay their last respects. Among the mourners were Ironsides and Terry H. Terry was muttering something out of the corner of his mouth and Ironsides was a little embarrassed because conversation is out of place at a time like that. But when he finally heard what Terry was saying, he nearly broke up and had great difficulty keeping quiet. Terry in fact had said, 'First fuckin' time he's been down below,' as they were lowering the coffin into the ground.

§

Jason and Ironsides were on nights at No. 3 Duke. There was whisky in the locker but the steel doors were padlocked. No watchman. 'Don't fuckin' worry,' said Jason. 'I'll get a bottle if it kills me.' With the aid of the steel bar he attacked the steel door, trying to detach it from its steel runners. Soon he was sweating and cursing but getting nowhere. Meanwhile, Ironsides was watching the proceedings with interest. His eyes wandered casually up to the ledge above the door where he saw the familiar shape of Bell's whisky bottles. Full. He watched Jason more in a lather then stopped him. 'Come over here a minute,' he said to Jason. 'Look up there,' said Ironsides. Jason saw the bottles on the ledge, and started swearing loudly. 'Why the fuck didn't you tell me they were there before?' he roared. They had been left by the Glasgow dockers.

§

Karate Kid was walking over the four bridges wearing a pair of stolen shoes. Lloydy and the Farmer's boy pulled him in for a routine search. Lloydy spotted the shoes and commented on them. Instead of staying cool, the Kid adopted a fighting stance and became very aggressive, threatening to chop them both. So he was promptly arrested and searched. In his wallet they found £70.

§

Big Joe F. was built like a telephone box. When he walked out with goodies not many policemen stopped him.

§

Saga of the most powerful binoculars in the world. The Leper, the Arab, Gummy and Joey B. were all sitting on the seawall at the Gladstone, idly watching the shipping and talking among themselves, at the same time eating tinned pears and pineapples. The Leper had somehow acquired a few tins of prawns. A couple of cargo ships were coming in about two miles away and speculation what and who they were was bandied about.

Joey: 'Wish I had my telescope now, I'd soon tell you what they were.'

Leper: 'Is it any good?'

Joey: 'Is it any good? It's bloody marvellous.'

Leper: 'Is it one of those on a stand?'

Joey: 'No. You can put this in your pocket. It's telescopic. I paid a fiver for it years ago.'

The Arab: 'Is it any fucking good?'

Joey: 'I don't buy rubbish. This is one of the best I've ever seen considering its size. I can sit in my front room and read the print of a newspaper someone is holding about two hundred yards away.'

Gummy: 'Takes some believing that.'

Leper: 'I'm not having that …'

The Arab: 'And neither am I …'

Joey (deeply hurt): 'I'm telling you the truth. Why should I lie?'

Leper: 'Not lying, Joey, just bending the truth a little.'

Arab: 'A fuckin' lot if you ask me.'

Gummy: 'Bring it in tomorrow and we'll see how fuckin' good it is.'

Joey: 'I will bring it tomorrow. You'll see. It's fuckin' marvellous.'

The next day they were back on the seawall during the welt. A few tins were opened and the Bartlett's went down a treat.

Leper: 'Right Joey, where's this marvellous telescope. Let's have a look at it.'

Joey took the telescope from one of his capacious overcoat pockets with a flourish. Gummy grabbed it quickly. 'Let's have a fuckin' shufti,' fiddling with the adjustings. 'Can't see fuck all …' he said.

Leper: 'Give it to me, ya blind bastard, the cover is still on …'

He takes it off and puts it to his eye. He looks over to the lighthouse off New Brighton. 'You were robbed, Joey. This is useless. I can see further without it.'

Joey: 'You're not using it properly.'
Leper: 'I fuckin' am. It's useless.'
The Arab: 'Throw it in the river and hang onto it.'

§

My Mother the Car, a holdsman, went to work in a Cortina and didn't believe in giving anyone a lift. This particular day it was absolutely teeming with rain. He saw some of the lads he knew who were working at the same ship waiting at a bus stop, and he knew they were going to be late booking on. He pulled up alongside them and wound his window down and spoke to them. 'Don't worry, lads; I'll tell the timekeeper you are on your way ...' and promptly wound up the window and took off.

§

Big A. and Sammy M. coming off the nights at No. 3 Duke were full of whisky and were well on as they left the ship, about 3 a.m. Staggering down the quay, they saw some Belgian fishing boats tied up. Sammy fancied some fish to take home but Big A. voted against the idea. 'These fuckin' fellers always carry knives, and I don't think they would like the idea of someone stealing their fish.' But Sammy was determined to have some so he crept aboard and grabbed about four large cod that were lying in a basket. Luckily he wasn't heard by any of the crew. He gave two to Big A. and they staggered home. Sammy arrived home, filled the sink, cleaned the fish up and, leaving them in the sink, went to bed. A few hours later he is awakened by loud screams as his wife sees the large lifeless eyes of the cod staring up at her.

§

Scarface Bob and I discovered some ingots in a China shed, but the snag was they were about three feet long and I knew they wouldn't fit in the boot of my mini. So they had to go on the rear seat, covered up with a coat, two at a time. But we managed to get about a dozen out.

§

We had a lorry parked up in a Clan shed this particular day, and were in the process of putting some copper reels on it, using a crane. The shed was full at the time and very busy. So we had plenty of cover. Or so we thought. Out of the blue came a police Land Rover, pulling up in front of us. There was no time to do anything except maybe have a heart attack. I remember telling all concerned to try and act natural, because for all they knew we could have been discharging the stuff. It was certainly a hairy moment. But luckily for us, the policemen jumped out and made straight for the ship. But we still put the copper on the lorry, only quicker.

§

I remember I could get seventy bottles of whisky in the boot of my little Mini. Sure, you could throw a case in and that would be it, but by emptying a few cardboard cartons and wrapping the bottles separately in newspaper, you could get much more in. Providing you have the time and the place to do it without being seen by nosey parkers or policemen. I know exactly how many because that is what I used to do. There were cars parked all over the place around the sheds. They didn't like you parking too near the sheds for obvious reasons. But sometimes you could park on the quay near the ship and there was always a large case you could get behind or at the side of. Just enough cover to do the business providing you had a mate with sharp eyes and you knew you could rely on him. The thing was never to get caught in the act or that was it. You could kiss your book goodbye.

J.D. and I were partners and worked well together. We used to take some small stuff like everyone else but when the opportunity arose we would take a few tons. Getting back to the whisky, we used to fill the boot up and then I would take the car near to the Pen and park it up. Go upstairs in the Pen and have a good look around through the windows with my binoculars. If there was anyone around I would forget about it for a while and then return later. From the Pen to get in the clear would take me roughly three minutes; by then I would be off the dock estate, but that didn't mean the danger was past. You could be pulled up within a short radius of the docks and searched. The police had a couple of unmarked vans they used but we knew all about them. They stood out like sore thumbs. We had all their numbers anyway. One of the dock police used his own car now and again and that stood out a mile too. In the late Sixties they even had a couple of Minis like mine but when you see two radio antennae on the rear you know who they are. One followed me off the dock estate one day. It was funny actually. In my rear view mirror I saw this policeman get all agitated when I drove past. I was empty at the time anyway. He couldn't get in his car fast enough. A much younger man was behind the wheel. He was pointing at me and I knew they were going to follow me. I know

I shouldn't have done it but I decided to have a little fun. I let them know I had seen them and took off like a jet. Actually they were held up a few seconds before they could get on my tail, so I waited down the dock road about three hundred yards. When I saw them come out of Duke Street gate, I got my foot down. We had a nice little run around the abandoned sheds in the four bridges area before I managed to jump in a line of traffic heading toward Seacombe. They couldn't follow. Just as well because they couldn't have done anything anyway.

§

The Great White Hunter (T.B.) was out hunting one day with a group of friends and he shot a swan. He always denied it but the name stuck. The Lazy Solicitor always seemed to struggle with a case. Lord Nelson would say, 'Keep your eye out for the boss.' The Sick Pigeon was always worked in the loft. The Plastic Surgeon was a good grafter. The Bobby Beater would say, 'Let's get stuck into this copper.' Telegram Boy would ask them to send more wires in. The Depth Charger would say, 'I'm going down for a sub.' Broken Clock said, 'Give us a lift; I've got a bad ticker.' Sick Lobster would say, 'Going home lads. One of me nippers is bad.' The Frightened Goalie would never go out for the net. Lino was always on the floor. Broken Boomerang would never come back. The Nudist would say, 'Bare thing suits me' (wouldn't work overtime). Park Keeper said, 'Mind the swing' (cargo swinging on the hook). Cecil Beaton was always taking photos. The Chauffeur was always running the boss to work. The Grandfather Clock was aptly named because he used to swing from side to side. Rocking Horse walked like one. Socks McCabe got caught with his socks on. Naked City jumped out of a bedroom window naked when the woman's husband came home unexpectedly.

One crane driver just didn't think about it when he said in all innocence, 'I've been to two berths today.' From then on he was stuck with the nickname Midwife. The Laughing Prince never seemed to smile.

§

Giggling Beetroot (Meals on Wheels, A.H.) was arrested one night pushing a pram along the dock road filled with toothpaste and soap. He was on his way to peddle it all. He was very lucky he was outside the docks when this happened otherwise he would have lost his book. The moral is don't booze when you want to do business. He was fined for his trouble.

§

Deaf Charlie, a watchman, didn't last long because he kept helping himself. We used to watch him filling his bag up with all sorts of goodies. We were sorry when he left but he was a bad example to us.

§

The Martian said, 'I'm going to me ma's for dinner.' Alfred Hitchcock was always saying, 'Put me in the picture, lads.' Aches and Pains was always complaining about his health. Cinderella commented, 'Got to be home for twelve, lads …' Electric Mouse was always dashing here and there. Wingless Chicken always had his hands in his pockets.

I remember a chap I worked with a few times down below. I gave him the nickname 'Spitting Cobra' as he had a habit of spitting quite often. Missed my boots several times. Filthy habit. Nice feller though.

Snarling Swede was one of the boys from the Clan days. Tall and well built, he looked like a Scandinavian but he always seemed to be snarling.

The Saturated Seven were Liverpool men who were always drunk, even on the 8 a.m. muster. The Busted Bale was another Liverpool man who got his nickname because of his appearance.

§

J.B. was one of the Three Wise Men. He put his sandwiches down on top of a 40-gallon drum on the quay and turned to say something to another docker. While his back was turned a flock of seagulls helped themselves to his butties. J.B. turned and saw them and said, 'Look at those fuckin' shitehawks, they'd eat anything.' Then he realised too late whose food they were eating …

§

One holdsman was very pigheaded. He would bet his life on the cheap and nasty wrist watch he wore. Swore Big Ben was very unreliable.

§

Men were sitting in the canteen one day having dinner in the company of Lemon Drop, who never stopped talking even when eating. One wag remarked, 'You don't need to buy a dinner where he is; he sprays everyone with food ...'

§

A hatch boss (who shall be nameless) used to get a little confused sometimes by the various names of the ports of call. Especially South Africa. Lourenço Marques, East London, Beira, Mozambique. The quay hands had to find out from him what was going into the ship. This particular day he was asked about some cargo that had to be stowed in the fo'c'sle head. These are special stowage and smaller type cases are sometimes stowed in there. But for some particular reason he thought the abbreviation for forecastle meant it was supposed to be going on a Castle boat.

§

One day a lorry driver jumped out of his cab dressed like a gun fighter from the Old West, complete with a gunbelt and holstered 45. 'I'm looking for this man they call the Lefthanded Gun. Where is he?' But the docker with this name wasn't available as he was on the mini shift.

§

Dave the Queer joined the Territorial Army. Turned in for work one morning dressed in his army uniform complete with stiff hat that practically covered his eyes.

§

Who could forget such memorable lines like these:

'Never mind the beams, lads; just put the hatch-boards on.' (This was from a hatch boss.)

Heard at a funeral: 'Never mind, Dad. We'll all be the same if God spares us ...' (This was the son at his father's funeral.)

At Big Norman's funeral there was some difficulty getting his coffin into the grave. A voice was heard to say, 'He never could measure a fuckin' case ...'

B.I. (hatch boss) had to ring another hatch boss to decide who was to go on nights. It was either him or the other man. The ship's boss left them to sort it out. So B.I. rang the other man at home to explain the situation to him and suggested they toss up. So they did over the phone, and B.I. told the other man he lost.

Another docker pulled back the corner of a tarp and a large dead rat fell out. He jumped back quickly saying, 'Fuckin' hell, this ship's alive with dead rats …'

§

Docker was telling his mates about the time he caught the lodger walking along the landing at his home, naked. 'I told him off because if my missus saw him like that, she would be very embarrassed.' Little did he know they were carrying on behind his back.

§

Mothercare, a holdsman, was on the mini shift. Around 10 p.m. the lads notice he was getting very agitated and asked him why. 'It's my lad,' he says, 'he won't go to bed if I don't give him a piggy back up the stairs …' The lads asked him how old he was. 'He's fifteen now,' he replied. Everyone fell about when they heard this.

Another time the same fifteen-year-old was fighting with another lad who threatened to bring his father. Mothercare told his lad that he couldn't fight the other man because, when they were both Teddy boys, they made a pact never to fight each other.

§

Big A. was boozing with a few friends in one of the crewmen's cabins on a Court Line tramp that was berthed at the Clan Line. Everything was great, singing and drinking, having a good time. Then one of the crew took a fancy to Big A. and tried to touch him up. But Big A. was against that sort of behaviour and took offence, grabbing the man and hurling him across the room. Of course, that broke the party up. This was witnessed by Jimmy C. … Happened on the nights at No. 3 Duke.

§

Charlie P. got slightly hurt down below. Brought out in a dirty, evil-smelling tub, but this wouldn't have bothered him. Taken to the hospital in an ambulance and then wheeled into the casualty department by the attendant. The sister came over to him and asked Charlie to take his boots off. Charlie looked surprised, 'They are off,' he replied.

§

Kenny B. (The Storyteller) had been everywhere, done everything.

'Yeah, I was in the Paras. Did thirty-two jumps.'

'Were you at Arnhem?'

'Too true. They were firing tracer at us coming down. A few rounds cut my shroud lines; I only just got down ...'

'You were in the Merchant navy too, weren't you?'

'Oh, yeah, all around the world on tramp steamers. One trip was two years. Out through the Panama and back through the Suez.'

'I heard you were in the Foreign Legion as well ... that right?'

'Sure was, did three years. Angola. Chad. Certainly get around in that mob. The worst time I had was in Indo-China ... Jesus ...'

'Not Dien Bien Phu?'

'I was never so scared in my life ... they never seemed to stop shelling us. Talk about sitting ducks ...'

'Were you taken prisoner?'

'In the end, yeah; had no choice. There were too many of them.'

'How long were you a prisoner?'

'About two years. When I eventually got home I took a heavy goods driving course and then went all over Europe. I got caught smuggling some hash in Syria and got three years. That's where I learned to speak fluent Arabic and French. You wouldn't believe the people in that place; still buying and selling dope. And forget about flush toilets ... just a hole in the ground.'

'You've certainly been around, Kenny ...'

This man Kenny B. just wasn't old enough to have been everywhere and done everything he claimed. He was a good grafter and very pleasant to work with, but some of his stories stretched credibility too far. We all wondered how he could keep his face straight. That was one thing he never claimed – that he had been a movie star in Hollywood. Or a brain surgeon.

§

Babs Davis was coming off the nights at the Chine. Staggering down the quay heading toward the gate, with a few other lads, all the worse for drink. They saw across the water some other dockers coming off a

Clan ship. So they started to take the piss, shouting things like 'Have a good night then? Plenty of whisky … ?' and having a good laugh.

The other dockers were in no mood because they had had nothing to drink. Insults were hurled back: 'Fuck off, you drunken bastards …'

One man shouted to Babs: 'Show us your arse then …'

Babs didn't hesitate. He dropped his trousers and bared his bottom to the other men across the water. But he didn't realise he was so near the edge and fell in with a loud splash … That broke everyone up right away.

§

Tommy W. had had too much whisky. He got out of the hatch somehow and collapsed on the quay. This was on the nights. His mates found him lying on top of a pallet board and decided to leave him where he was, so they threw an old tarpaulin over him to keep him warm. This happened about 4 a.m. Somehow they forgot all about him and left the ship at 7 a.m. and went home. The day shift came on at 8 a.m. and some men were working in the area where Tommy was sleeping it off. Then he decided to make a move and stirred. He arose like a ghost throwing the tarpaulin from him, causing instant panic to the other men, who scattered quickly.

§

Smelly F. was on the days at the China and was legless down below (too much firewater). The lads had to send a tub in to get him out of the hatch. Usually a man will accompany someone in the tub, but this time there were no volunteers because he stunk. Billy E. and Billy O. were in the gang. Eventually someone went with him and they got him on the quay. Then they had to get a taxi to take him home. When they arrived Smelly was in more trouble. His wife poured a bucket of water over him and then jammed the bucket over his head and kept striking the bucket with an iron bar …

§

The Dummy. This chap started on the docks and was warned by his father, who incidentally had worked on the docks for years, not to say or do anything foolish that would earn him a nickname. So he kept his mouth shut most of the time. Because he wouldn't say anything he got this name. You cannot win.

§

Jackie T. was working with the Hungry 8 at Brock's, including Long Larry, the Dumper. All down below as usual. They were sitting in the wings of the tween deck waiting for a sling to come in. Jackie was puffing away on a cigarette quite happy. Suddenly the familiar polished boots and blue twill legs came into view coming down the ladder. The police were checking the hatches, looking for a docker they suspected of stealing and who had run off when called. He had run onto this ship and eluded them.

It was obvious the suspect wasn't here but the sergeant decided to have a go at Jackie. 'You've been smoking, haven't you?' pointing an accusing finger at the stumps on the deck.

Jackie looked hurt. 'Not me, sarge. We're not allowed to smoke down a hatch. Think I'm stupid?'

'You were smoking. Don't lie to me. Don't think I'm stupid,' retorted the Policeman going red in the face. Things began to get heated.

'Why don't you just fuck off,' said Jackie. 'To think I lost some blood on the beach at Dunkirk for the likes of you ...'

The sergeant was fuming by now and banging his baton on a case. 'You never lost any blood for me,' he shouted. 'I want your name now.'

The other men were trying not to fall about at this carry-on.

Finally Jackie told him his name because the policeman only had to see the timekeeper to find out who was down the hatch. He had been at Dunkirk, been bombed and shot at on the beach. So a fine of three pounds for smoking in a prohibited area was small potatoes for Jackie. And they never found the other man.

He had been in a worse situation at another ship when he overbalanced and fell 20 feet among some men working below. One wag was heard to say, 'Who sang out for a make-up?' Poor Jackie suffered some broken bones in a heel.

§

J.D. and I got four huge compressors away from the Golden Mile one day. Had to use a crane to get them off the deck and onto a trailer.

While we were doing it, a certain quay foreman was seen strolling along, coming toward us. We knew this man wouldn't hesitate to call the police if he thought there was something going on. So we had to hide until he had gone past. We watched him look at our trailer and then carry on. Then we waited a few minutes just to see if he would do anything. We knew the value of the load was £27,000. We got it safely away but we found out later our contact down the motorway had blown it. Two days later we saw the compressors coming back on another trailer. We were choked, naturally.

We were standing in the avenue and J.D. saw the load coming in from the M53. 'I don't want to upset you, Len, but that certainly looks like our lot coming back …' He was right. It had been recovered and was being returned. Don't know exactly what happened, but we lost that one. This time they were taken into the shed and put in the cage with a watchman.

Another time we lost 40 tons of steel plate from the same place; this was recovered too. And then another 20 tons of angle iron. This was getting too much for us, but we persevered a little longer. Still on the Golden Mile, we put three tractors on a trailer with the help of a stacker truck. Then we put the huge tyres on top and secured them. We helped the driver put a sheet over and then rope it. All the while we were doing this, we had to watch no one was sneaking up on us and catching us in the act. Of course, we employed a couple of the lads to keep watch at certain points we considered dangerous. Finally we completed the load. But the engine of the artic stopped. He had kept it running because his battery was on the blink. So now, here we are with a fully laden truck of stolen goods, broken down on the dock estate. So we borrowed a crane and used it to push him just enough to jump start his truck, and off he went. We thought that was that, but we were in for another shock. Twenty minutes later the driver returns on foot to tell us he has broken down in some street. Jesus! He shouldn't have been in any street. He should have been on the motorway. I walked back with him to see where he had broken down. For some reason he has taken the wrong turning. Why, I don't know, because all he had to do was get straight on the main road and he would have been on the M53 in a matter of minutes. When I saw his vehicle, I nearly flipped. He had stalled it on a slight incline and allowed it to roll back so that the rear of the truck was a few feet away from the corner of a house! If he had released the handbrake, it would have demolished part of the house. The driver didn't seem to be with it, so I had to take some action.

First we had to find something to put under his rear wheels to choc them. I don't think it would have done much good, because the load was heavy and the slight incline didn't help us. But we found some bricks and put them under the wheels. It was a very dangerous predicament to be in. A police car could come past any minute, or a nosy neighbour might ring them. When we thought the vehicle was secure, I had to go and rang a local contact who owned some vehicles to send one of his to come and tow our vehicle up this side street and away. We had to wait about thirty minutes and it seemed like an eternity. But all went well and that was one round we won. I dread to think what would have happened if the truck had hit the corner of the house.

Another time, J.D. and I had just put 20 tons of steel plate on a trailer we had borrowed. The tractor unit was due in about an hour, so we nipped into the nearby dock canteen for a cuppa. We were sitting there all made up. We could see the trailer just outside. Along comes H.M., the quay foreman, who looked at it in surprise. He jumped up and checked the port marks and decided something fishy was going on. We were watching with bated breath until he gave the order to have it taken into the ship right away. So all our hard work was for nothing. I spoke to H.M. years later and mentioned this to him. I told him he had done us out of a lot of money; I was only joking, of course. But he surprised me by saying, 'Why didn't you tell me? Things could have been arranged.' We laugh at it now. I still see him every week. The things he told me. I only wish I had known.

§

Nights at a Harrison ship, Bidston Dock. The Leper, Ray the Liar, Harry Worth, Les S. and me were down No. 2 and there was all sorts going but Les and I filled a sack up with shoes. All leather, and different sizes. We managed to get the sack along the deck without being seen to the fo'c'sle head. There was too much activity around the other hatches to risk throwing it onto the quay, plus everywhere was floodlit. So we were up on the fo'c'sle head where it was quiet and fairly dark. We got some rope yarns and tied them together forming a long line. Then we tied the sack of shoes to it. Our man was on the quay ready to receive it. There were about thirty pairs of shoes in the sack. There was a wide gap between the ship and the quay and I was beginning to have doubts about reaching the quay, but we tried anyway. We got a good swing on the rope and it was looking good. Until the rope snapped and the sack fell in the water. That meant the shoes were ruined anyway. We were horrified at the waste, but we had to retrieve the sack and dispose of the evidence.

§

J.D. and I had a hairy time one day. We had brought a friend in who had parked his articulated vehicle on the quay at the Clan. Our target was a length of steel shaft, similar to a prop shaft in a ship. We knew it was special steel and we had a buyer for it; it was just over twenty feet in length. So we needed a crane driver to pick it up for us and place it on our truck. Our friend Humpty Dumpty jumped at the chance to make a few shillings. Everything was looking great. The truck was set up near the water's edge, and Humpty was between the truck and the shed. We put the wires on each end, with wood in the eye to stop them sliding. We were ideally situated, away from prying eyes, but we still kept a sharp lookout. There was nothing to stop a police van coming out of any of the shed gates, or coming down either end of the key. But sometimes you have to take chances. And you always need luck. We hooked up and Humpty took the weight, and that's when our troubles started. The crane started to topple over, so he had to lower it immediately. The shaft was heavier than we thought. Meanwhile, Humpty is sweating profusely. And then the radiator sprung a leak and steam escaped everywhere. And to top it all, we saw one of the head men walking down the quay towards us …

This man was a bastard and would shop his own mother. Our driver remained cool all the time. Not so Humpty. He wanted to flee. I had to convince him to stay and bluff it out, because Dangerman was not to know the shaft was coming off the truck to be stowed on the quay. But J.D. and I had to hide because we were known. So we got under the truck and watched him come closer. Humpty had left the crane to get some water for the radiator. Dangerman could see what the trouble was and started to give suggestions, but this only made Humpty sweat more. But to give him his due, he didn't crack up. Dangerman looked all around as if he couldn't make his mind up about something; we could see him from where we were hiding. Eventually he moved off and went into the shed. We complimented Humpty on his nerve, but he could hardly speak – he was still in shock.

We eventually loaded the shaft onto the truck and secured it, and off we went out of the gate. It finished up in North Wales. It was a fairly happy ending for all, except Humpty. Because the next day the shaft was missed. Dangerman was back on the scene accusing Humpty of stealing it. He was arrested. Of course, he denied vehemently having anything to do with it. Dangerman wanted him jailed, but they couldn't prove anything, and Humpty was in the clear. He felt a lot better when he was rewarded for his pains. He asked us to go easy on him the next time, as he couldn't take the pressure.

§

Billy S. was a good bagman. Would take anything. But he never liked the Alfred Dock. Thought it was too much like a rat trap. But one day he allowed himself to be persuaded against his better judgement and took a chance with some good cloth. It wasn't his lucky day because the Farmer and Lloydy were there. They caught him on the lock gates. 'Got you now, Billy,' they gloated. That was the end of Billy's days on the docks.

I believe he used to go past them and whistle and pat his cloth-bound body and pedal like mad. They used to wait for him outside his house, and Billy would say to them, 'You don't think I'm that fuckin' soft, do ya? Wanna come in and have a look?'

Lloydy said to him, 'OK, Billy, but my mate's around the back just in case …'

'That's all right,' Billy said, 'come in. Wanna cup of tea, or maybe coffee?'

He was at the East Quay once at a ship in the locker loading whisky. The Mate, a watchman and the cadet were also in the locker watching the loading. Someone said to Billy, 'No fuckin' chance here …' They finished loading the whisky, the locker was locked and the Mate and the others went up out of the hatch. Somehow Billy had taken four bottles from under their noses. The hatch boss Freddie W. was offered a bottle but declined as he said his wife would smash it over his head if she thought it had been stolen.

§

All the boys were having a good drink down below. Two gangs were working at the same hatch. There was a bight between the two parts of the hatch, one gang working each. They usually threw some kind of cargo down there later, like bags. Mumbling Mick (a holdsman) was well on by this time and took off like an express train for some reason, falling into this bight. Billy the Goalkeeper took him home in a car with the help of Ronnie H. after he had been taken out in a net. Mick's legs were slightly hurt in the fall but he never felt a thing. They arrived at Mick's house and supported him to the front door. Mick's wife took one look and started hitting Mick over the head with her shoe, saying, 'Where the fuck's his bike … ?'

§

Cathcart Street, China berth. Electric bogie went in the dock. The diver went down to recover it. Meanwhile, about a dozen dockers gathered round to see what was going on. Most of them were standing on the save all to get a better view. Suddenly, a rope parted, and into the dock they all went. I believe the diver, who was on his way up, couldn't understand what was happening when he saw all these bodies thrashing around in the water. I believe you could hear the laughter all the way up to the Bidston Dock.

§

A gang was working down below with a watchman who was daft enough to admit he was terrified of rats. Jimmy D., Willo and G.B. decided to have some fun. They got a short piece of rope with a frayed end and made it look like a rat and put it between the watchman's legs. Then someone shouted a warning about a rat running around. The poor fellow saw it and promptly fainted. The lads were a little upset at this and were concerned but luckily the watchman came round.

§

I was going out the gate one day on my scooter, a Lambretta. I had two pairs of leather shoes hidden in the engine cowling. As I passed the policeman on point duty, he pointed to the scooter and I saw smoke coming from it. I just waved and kept going as I knew what it was. When I got safely out of the way and out of view I pulled up and took the cowling off and saw the shoes smouldering away. I had to dump them because they were ruined.

§

I was going down the quay at the Bidston Dock driving a stacker with a five-hundredweight case of copper on the forks. J.D. was with me walking alongside. We were on our way to a skip in which we were going to dump the case to be taken out later. We passed the ship's boss, who looked at us and just shook his head and got out the way. I was alongside the ship and about to go into the shed and out the other side to where the skip was situated. Out the shed door walked two well-known dock policemen, Lloydy and the Farmer's Boy. Both looked at me hard as they went aboard the ship and up the gangway. I just couldn't jump off and run – that would have suited them, so I stayed put and carried on. I felt their eyes boring into my back as I went into the shed. I daren't look at them, so J.D. kept me informed as to what they were doing. They carried on into the ship's accommodation and we carried on. Lloydy should have known I had no right on a stacker. He knew I worked down below. If I had been him, I would have known.

§

Shit on the Deck, Little J.F. and the Naked Runner were working together at the North Quay. They managed to take a vanload of micro-ovens from the quay. They were stashed by the Runner but later had vanished. The others wanted to know where, and J.F. pinned him to the shed wall. The Runner explained that he had to get rid of them quickly as the police were onto him. It was obviously a put-up story, so J.F. pinned the Runner to the shed wall again and said, 'I'll kick you all round the fuckin' quay if you don't tell us the truth.'

The Runner said, 'And I know you are just the man to do it …'

§

Fiddler on the Roof had a load of stolen cloth hidden away in his loft. The police called to search and he was seen on the roof. He stayed there for a while but came down and was arrested. When the hatch boss we called Drug Addict shouted down the hatch, it sounded like he was saying, 'I've got a bit more for ya [morphia].' Seacombe Lover was grabbed by the PLO for nights. He almost had a heart attack. 'What? Me? Fuck off. I don't do nights. Nights are made for loving.' The Gardener would say, 'Let's plant ourselves here …' Jealous Husband always asked, 'Where's the other man?' The Handbag was always carried by his mates. Mangy Cat was thrown out of every yard. The Senator was always in the White House (wine lodge). Machine Gun fired out his words at eight hundred a minute.

§

The Whippet was working on a Maru boat on Mortar Mill quay. In the lower hold was stowed the Aston Martin DB used by James Bond in the movies. Ritchie had been sampling Beefeater Gin and Vat 69 and was rotten. He was attempting to get down into the hold when he fell from the ladder and his legs jammed into the steel rungs, breaking one and fracturing the other. So he was hanging upside down for a while until help came. The usual thing is to get back on the quay and put in a claim. But a certain ship's boss who shall be nameless (Big N.) put the blocks on that idea right away. So the Whippet had six months off work while he recovered.

The same man, working at a Clan boat, opened a case to see what was in it and discovered it was full of tableware, silver cutlery, and it was the best. So he took it. Later on, he discovered it was a special consignment going to Karachi especially to be used by the Queen on her tour. Visions of ending up in the Tower flashed through his mind momentarily but didn't make him return it.

Another time, he took six bottles of whisky home and put them in a bucket containing dirty nappies when the police knocked on his door. He already had another six bottles in the spin drier. They came in to search but never found any.

§

We had a furniture van in one day, backed into a corner of the shed where they stored the fine goods. Hard to believe but there wasn't any watchman at that time. The quay foreman had conveniently gone for a drink to get himself out of the way for about half an hour. J.D., two others and I handballed all sorts of stuff into the back of it right away. The hired driver stowed it as soon as we passed it to him. Kitchenware, utensils, cutlery, pottery, crockery, tools, small carpets. Everything was going well. We had lookouts posted to watch out for the head of security, Mr B. Then the driver started cracking up. By this time we had the van over half full. He wanted to pack up and go but we managed to calm him down. Then we could see he was going to blow, so we asked him to take three pallet boards of salmon and then call it a day. He reluctantly agreed so we quickly got hold of a stacker and put the salmon in. He couldn't shut the doors quick enough. We had really sweated throwing the stuff in. We knew for a fact the salmon was worth three thousand pounds. We got him out of the dock estate safely and were quite pleased with our efforts. But not so pleased a few days later.

§

When we had to heave case cars into the wings, someone had to climb the stringers with a Bulldog grip; this was a lump of iron weighing around ten pounds shaped like a small vice. This was secured to one of the deck-head plates. Then it was tightened with a piece of wood to try and stop it sliding when a block was attached and the runner rove through it for the deckhand to start heaving to try and drag a large case into the wing, These runners have been known to part like a violin string, so you have to keep well out of the way. We had to leave a Bulldog one time as it was impossible to retrieve because of the pressure put on it.

When a Clan ship came in to be loaded it usually took about ten days, maybe less if there was a night shift working. I didn't particularly like the nights, but if you were with a good gang it was far better and time went quickly enough. Good mates made all the difference; you knew you could trust them. In your time off, you could stay down below and get your head down on top of a case with your head on a coat. Summer it was OK but winter made a big difference of course. Then you could either go to a mess room or the engine room casing, until we were chased by an engineer. Sometimes down below there could be cartons to lie on, or even carpets in the cargo. As I mentioned, we once built a little cave with cartons and rolled up carpets for a pillow.

Reminds me of reading about the car makers Vauxhall in Ellesmere Port; they actually had secret rooms where they even had a TV (this was the night workers). We drew the line at having a TV. So this is the way on the docks.

The ordinary man in the street would have no idea of the size of a ship's hatch, especially No. 2, which is usually the biggest hatch on the ship. You could get two or three double-decker buses or two or three railway engines or locomotives or two or three hundred cars in there. Then there are upper tween decks to be filled with cargo.

One afternoon on a City boat on the Golden Mile. Jimmy the Donkey, Birdman, the Suitcase and I were stowing bags of cement in the lower hold, into the wings, and we had to go as high as the deck-head. We had nearly finished and the boss told us to expect a stacker because we were going to get some heavy cases which were to go across the hatch longer for longer until we came out to the square. So we had a lie down until the stacker came in; it could be quite a while. Suitcase got his Louis L'Amour western out. Suddenly a shout from the deck: 'Stand in below; stacker coming in …'

'Fucking hell,' said the Suitcase, 'is there no fucking peace around here? What's the fuckin' hurry?'

'Well. we do have to show willing and get the ship loaded; after all, this isn't a fuckin' library,' offered the Birdman sarcastically.

The stacker was landed and the four wires unshackled and held until the fall took it up. Scarface Bob was climbing down the ladder and came over: 'Right lads, who's the lucky man who is going to let me go for a bevvy or two?'

Jimmy volunteered.

'No fuckin' chance,' said Harry; 'you forgettin' you nearly fuckin' killed us on the dock road?'

'Give him a chance,' said Suitcase. 'He should be OK on the stacker … he can't kill anyone down here …'

'Wanna fuckin' bet?' said Harry. 'Anyway, it's nearly three o'clock – the others are due back. Let them sort it out.'

Two of the other gang came back on time. Paleface Harry was first down followed by the Whistling Kettle. Kettle always wore a silk cravat but when he whistled no sound came out. Strange. The other two lads turned up but one was the worse for wear; he managed to get down and staggered into the wings. This did not look good. Harry warned us the Manager was on the quay near the gangway talking to the ship's boss. He probably saw Harry and his mate coming back to the ship. Bob had no chance of slipping away unless someone volunteered to drive the stacker; besides, the Manager would probably come around with the timekeeper. So we made our way onto the main deck and skulked around the winches till the coast was clear. If the Manager came near we would have to get below quickly until he saw everything was in order and left the ship, and we would follow him until he disappeared into the shed.

This is what went on sometimes but not always. You could go to a ship that would be filling a whole hatch with drums of caustic soda and that meant all eight men would possibly have to stay below. Four men on one side of the hold and the other four men on the other. The drums would come in four or eight at a time. Then we would unhook the chains and start rolling them in and head them up. Later they discovered it wouldn't do any harm to leave them on their rolling way, thus saving us a lot of backbreaking work. Loading hundreds of these drums would take a week or so unless they put a night shift on. It could get boring with this kind of cargo, but if you had good mates and could have a laugh, the time soon went. We might get a few extra shillings for all this tonnage. Now compare it with the following.

A Clan ship, the *MacTaggart*, had a new derrick fitted with an outreach of twenty feet with a heel of ten degrees, and the complete outfit had a weight of 205 tons. Her new addition was tested to near limit when a 160-ton stator was loaded at Birkenhead for South Africa in 1964. It was said these enhanced freight charges earned when carrying heavy loads to Australia paid for the whole voyage with the homeward trip pure profit … the men who picked it up from the *Mammoth* crane and the men down the hatch to place the heavy balks of timber were paid a lot more for less work. But you were very lucky to get picked from the Pen. But that was the luck of the draw. Same with the billet ships that came to Rea's Wharf to load or discharge heavy loads. This was where you got big money for less work. I went there once and it paid buttons.

§

On nights at No. 3 Duke. Safmarine ship. Down No. 1 with Friday Frank, Big Geoff, Spiderman. Porthole Pete was the hatch boss. The first thing we noticed was the locker in the fore part, steel doors padlocked. Right away I saw the dollar signs. We used the fall to pull the lock off. I remember the steel door nearly came off as well. Now and again they slipped up by not putting a watchman down below or didn't think it was necessary. We were lucky both ways. We didn't have a spare lock to put on so we had to replace the mangled one and hoped for the best. We carried a load ashore and hid it in a field just across the road. A certain man working on the quay offered to help us carry our loot and keep watch for us. We told him to fuck off. Nobody liked him anyway. We all hid our own whisky in little piles in this field; it was really a patch of waste ground overgrown with grass and bushes. The next morning leaving the ship at 7 a.m. we took our own and headed for home and bed. Then we were given the news the ship was working Saturday night. This is called the Golden Nugget. I remember a few men refusing, but they had their reasons. Saturday night there was a little trouble. Frank booked on full of booze. Geoff and I were talking on the fo'c'sle head when Frank approached us in a very belligerent mood, almost accusing us of stealing his whisky. I resented his attitude and told him so. He threatened Geoff, but I managed to pacify him and told him who had probably taken his whisky. I had noticed the creep on the quay watching us one morning making a trip across the avenue. It was probably him anyway – it was his style. So I told Frank all about it. This chap was late booking on and Frank waited for him. When he did eventually arrive, Frank hit him, blacking his eye. Served him right.

§

J.D. and some friends were in a railway wagon this particular day, which was parked alongside the ship on the quay. They were helping themselves to some goodies inside. Batman was outside keeping watch, or was supposed to. Suddenly the Law arrived after getting a tip off, and Batman took off like a bat out of Hell, never even giving the lads inside a warning. Luckily, a sharp-eyed docker saw the Law and shouted, 'Paddy Kelly.' This was the word that warned everyone that the police were around. If it hadn't been for this late warning, they would have all been caught red-handed, but as it was, they jumped out and ran for their lives.

I have seen men with ten bottles of whisky hidden about their person still look normal. Others just couldn't hide the fact they were carrying something; they looked positively lumpy. Six bottles was my limit, and even then I felt very conspicuous. Some of the articles I have taken needed a lot of careful handling. Especially bone china ornaments, the tips of wings or a wing, or even a beak could break easily and the article would be useless. I remember one time getting some beautiful elephants out. They had their trunks raised, so they needed careful handling. China tea sets, cutlery, kitchen utensils – I have taken the lot. Even can openers, mirrors, bottles of perfume, packets of Durex condoms.

If we were working down below and it started to rain heavily, we would be told to get up and cover the hatch. If there was something worth taking, and there was a watchman, we would try and remain behind, hidden, because the watchman would have to get out of the hatch also. By the time the rain had stopped we would have had our loot ready to take from the ship. A torch was always handy when this happened, because it was extremely dangerous in a dark hatch. I have known of men who have stayed down below all night just to get some stuff. A blanket and thermos was handy when this happened. But you needed good nerves to do this. If the hatch was battened down and mast-house locked, you had no chance to get out until the next morning. But you had to be careful you were not spotted by any of the ship's crew or officers. If there were night gangs working, it was different. Some men working days would turn up on the mini shift at 11 p.m. to carry off. I did this just once.

§

Sometimes the crane driver had to have a docker guiding the cargo on the end of his hook around certain parts of the shed, because it was extremely difficult for the driver to negotiate the bends and corners of the cargo laid down on the deck. The mobile cranes that were used in the sheds to get the cargo to the ship's side were heroes. They had a terrible job. They had to have the patience of a saint to do their job, and a head that could turn 360 degrees. Davy C. was a well-known character at this particular job, but he was inclined to fly off the handle sometimes.

Crane drivers were constantly turning and reversing, working the jib of the crane up and down. One of the sheds on the Golden Mile was over a hundred years old, and to get into the shed, the jib had to be lowered almost horizontal to get through the door because of the headroom. Davy C. forgot to lower his jib one time and hit the top and loads of bricks came tumbling down. Of course, when something like that happens, when someone might in all innocence ask Dave what happened, his stock answer was always the same. 'How the fuckin' hell do I know?' It was always wise not to argue with him because he was very volatile. What a character.

One day he was coming down the avenue on the Golden Mile, with a very long Stanton pipe on his hook, very expensive too. It had a large circumference and was wanted for a very special job abroad. Something happened along the way and the pipe touched the ground and became unhooked. It hit the ground, smashing into a few hundred pieces. The ship's boss happened to see the accident and nearly had a fit. He came over to Davy on the warpath. 'What happened, Davy?' he asked offensively.

'How the fuckin' hell do I know what happened, ya thick twat,' answered Davy.

The boss got lost very quickly. Another time, Davy got the jib of his crane caught in the low beams supporting the roof in Brock's old shed. No matter what he did, it held fast and stayed like that for a couple of hours. It caused a lot of merriment with the lads, Davy slowly getting worked up at the snide comments from the onlookers. 'Losin' your touch, Davy?' 'Bevvied are we?' 'Going fuckin' blind, Davy?' 'Glad we are down below with you on the quay ...'

S.M. was ugly. Some unfeeling docker said his mother used to feed him through a wire mesh fence ... One morning in the Pen he was heard to say about a new intake, 'Lots of new faces here ...' Quick as a flash, Sid E. snapped, 'Yeah, well why don't you fuckin' get one ...'

Another time, Davy was hurtling down the shed with some steel pipes on his hook. Something happened and the end of the pipes burst through the office window, shattering the glass. The clerks inside jumped for their lives thinking a bomb had gone off. Someone was stupid enough to ask him what happened. And got the classic answer, 'How the fuckin' hell do I know?'

Billy S., another crane driver, was taking the beams off using a dockside crane. It was just after 8 a.m. and the ship's officers were just settling down at the breakfast table below the bridge when the end of the beam came smashing through a porthole, shattering the glass. After that incident Billy was known as Beams on Toast.

One time he was dragging a very expensive Stanton pipe, used for underground sewage, when it hit the ground and fell off the hook and broke into pieces. No one dared go near Davy because they knew what he would say.

§

Elliot Ness (George E.), a timekeeper at Rea's Wharf, had a fabulous memory for numbers. One of the lads was heard to say, 'Bastard, never forgets a number ...'

'Rubber' Wilson, also a timekeeper at Rea's, was dead keen. He went over and above the normal call of duty. A man was injured down below and in a bad way. He was also in shock. They were taking him to the ambulance on a stretcher and Rubber was seen hovering above him like a vulture asking, 'What's your number? What's your number?' The injured man could hardly speak never mind remember his number.

§

A holdsman was working over in Liverpool at the Toxteth. The Dutch ship was also carrying tulip bulbs which were destined for the UK. He was among six other men stopped at the gate and taken in to be searched. While the others were being searched, he ate the bulbs he was carrying.

§

Lenny S. managed to swipe half a dozen shoes from the display in the Boot Van. But the snag was they were all for one foot only. So he took them in the Amenity Block and asked the cleaner there did he want to buy any shoes. Genuine leather. The cleaner was made up to be offered a bargain. Lenny asked him to choose any of them.

'How much do you want for them?' the cleaner wanted to know.

'Give us a pound and you can take your pick of any of them,' said Lenny.

The cleaner tried a nice brown shoe on and it fitted perfectly. 'Are you sure you only want a pound?' he asked.

Lenny smiled and said, 'No, I don't want a pound. You can keep that one ...'

§

Two dockers were going out the gate at Duke Street. One man could hardly walk because of the cloth he had wrapped around him. He looked like Humpty Dumpty. The policeman on point duty must have thought he was seeing things and got down from his box to search him. He was just about to grab him when the other docker quickly dropped his trousers exposing his backside and other parts to the public. There were buses passing and cars and everyone was getting an eyeful.

Motorists were honking and people shouting. The policeman had no choice, so he grabbed the naked docker and arrested him. During the confusion his mate got away.

§

You could go to a ship hoping for the best as regards the bag. But you could finish up with nothing but a strained back. But some ships there was always something. Might not be much but at least it was something. For instance, I went to a Pakistani ship once at the East Quay and it was all hard work. But also down the hatch was a bale of tea towels and curtain material. So after each welt I helped myself and carried a few off at a time. It all helped to supplement my earnings. But as I said, this method was like playing Russian roulette. After all, the items were only worth a few pounds, but taken in large quantities over a week it mounts up to a considerable sum. The ship in front of you might be having something better going but that's the way it went. You sometimes would get an invite down someone else's hatch, but this was bad practice really. If there is a watchman down there, he won't like all the strange faces coming and going. Obviously it increases the chances of discovery and then his head will roll. I have taken bottles of whisky out of the hatch just to stop other nosey bastards coming down and spoiling everything. And that did happen. Some selfish bastard would start poking his nose over the coaming and shouting down to a mate. You had to try and keep it a secret if you got something down below but most times it was impossible because some of those deckhands and quay hands would smell a rat if they saw you making a few trips up and down the quay. They could easily tell if you were carrying something. Especially if they saw your head turning a full 360 degrees as you were walking. There was an expression on the docks about some men using a burglar's coat. Plenty of pockets and long. They had to be fairly strong those pockets. I have tied the ends of my sleeves and filled them with bottles of whisky and walked out the gate with the coat over my arm. I never liked carrying whisky and the most was five at a pinch. Once they were in place you could not bend at all. Another reason was if you were approached by a policeman you could throw your coat into the dock if you were near enough. Some men I knew could carry eight bottles around their waist and secured by a leather belt. And to look at some of them you wouldn't think they weren't carrying at all. Funny when you are walking along and the man in front of you is carrying and a bottle slips out and smashes on the ground. The only thing you can do is keep walking and get away from there as fast as you can. Or you could wait to see another docker getting dragged into the policeman's hut or building to be searched, and you quicken your own pace to get past quick. It seems lousy but it had to be done, and he would have done the same.

§

Sometimes when we broke into a case down below, we did our best to try and hide the evidence. Broken and splintered wood, wire bands, packing paper. For instance, if we broke into a case from the side, we would turn it completely round. Or from the top we would just turn the case over once – that was enough. Or if, by chance, the case was completely destroyed, we would throw the remains down the ship's side, the stringers. But if there was nowhere to hide the pieces safely, we would send it ashore to be disposed of there. The watchman would only have to see a piece of cardboard, or a wrapper, and that meant trouble. If we had found some goodies down below and if we didn't want anyone else to know, we would try and relocate it. If we knew for a fact there were night men coming on, we would go all out to try and get it away or relocate it before we finished work. But sometimes it was too much for us and we had no choice but to let them find it. On the other hand, there was a chance the others might not be interested. But not very often. There were always one or two who were bag-men. As I have stated, we were not all thieves. No matter how well we covered our tracks, there were men who had eyes like a shit house rat and would spot clues Sherlock Holmes would miss ... It's funny when you think about it. We seemed to think that it actually belonged to us, and no one else had any right to take it. Sometimes when a ship came to Birkenhead from around the land, like Swansea, or Cardiff, or Glasgow, we would find evidence that these dockers from other ports had been busy. We would even find full bottles of whisky hidden away in various hiding places. And if anyone in Security started sniffing around and found 'our' whisky we would immediately throw all the blame on these other dockers. I might add also that when some ships arrived here from other ports in the UK, their stowage of part cargo left a lot to be desired. Nine times out of ten, we had to restow some of it. I remember a Clan ship coming around from Swansea with part cargo in the lower hold, looking like a Mad Hatter's tea party. So before anything else was sent in, we had to restow it. It was that bad. I have myself said, 'Fuck it, leave it where it is' about a certain case or commodity, but I knew it wouldn't do any harm to leave this as it was. In the case of bags, it was different. Where you had hundreds of bags to stow in the lower hold (and sometimes in the tween decks) we used to leave a huge space. If we didn't feel like walking in too far, we used to go so far and build a wall right across the hatch, leaving a blank space behind. This was known as a Glasgow Wall. At the same time we had to hit the deck-head to prevent anyone discovering the space behind.

This wasn't a dangerous practice by any means; it was just sheer laziness on our part. We had to do it quickly before the boss should come down and see what was going on. But sometimes we would come unstuck if he saw what was going on, and order us to do the job properly. Then we would have no option but to do as ordered. Sometimes the wall came down if the cartons, bags or whatever weren't stowed correctly. But it was completely different when two gangs were down the hatch and it was split in half. One gang forward, the other aft. Sometimes we had to fill completely the lower hold with bags. The other gang might be loading steel, or such other heavy cargo. Then we would have to build a bulk-head from the deck, right up to the tween deck. Our face had to be fairly straight, just like a brick wall. So someone had to have a good eye. Also it was fairly dangerous working two gangs down the same hatch because there would be two falls working all the time.

Many a time I have been working and heard a shout, 'Stand in below,' and leapt for cover only to discover it was the other gang's deckhand. You could be working on bags and be about 20 feet up in the air and the other gang still on the deck. They used to put a rope across the hatch as a safety precaution. But this was pretty useless, as it would never stop you falling if you overbalanced. It was there mainly as a reminder of the danger. That was the beauty of the job, as I have said, plenty of variety. Even if the job was utterly boring, you could still have a laugh if you had the right mates. But if by any chance you should be sent as a make-up to a gang whose outlook differed from yours, you could be in for a miserable time. For example, I was sent as a make-up to a gang who didn't believe in the welt. Also we had a stacker down below and only two men were needed really, but they still didn't like the idea of any men going away. All you can do in those circumstances is grin and bear it, or sleep in the next day. This only happened to me one time fortunately. Another time I had the misfortune to work with two notables, Hercules and the Silver Bullet. Both needed operations to remove their hands from their pockets. I never did find out how men could stow heavy cases, Stanton pipes, bags, all done with no hands. I did, however, see a foot getting used now and then. I have seen men actually talk a heavy case into the wings … this takes some doing as you can imagine. Then you can get what we used to call a yard arm lift.

This entails a man leaning against the bulk-head with one hand, and half-heartedly using the other to drag the case in ...

§

During my career on the docks, I saw a lot of things happening that would have really shocked you. But when it happened we just grinned and tried again. For instance we would be heaving a car in, completely encased in a large wooden case. The order would be given after the blocks had been placed in position and the wires sorted out, 'OK, start heaving ...' and the man on the deck would take his orders from the man watching the proceedings down below. Remember, the deckhand cannot see what is going on most of the time. He watches the man below giving a hand signal. This means using a system known to the deckhand. A beckoning gesture using all the fingers together, like the opening and closing of the hand. This means HEAVE. The flat of the hand similar to a policeman putting up his hand with the palm out means what it says: STOP. Or sometimes the holdsman will use only one finger, again a beckoning gesture meaning HEAVE. If he closes his fist that also means STOP. The man below had to have very good judgement and give the deckhand plenty of time to relay it to the crane-driver or winchman. Sometimes the deckhands would have to reposition the derricks to get certain types of cargo placed in the hatch. The derrick might have to be topped or lowered, moved to left or right; guys have to be adjusted and the preventers also. Sometimes the wire runner from the barrel on the winch had to be run off and rerun back on to take a kink out, as this could be very dangerous. Just like an aeroplane hitting an air pocket. There is a sudden drop. In the plane, it doesn't matter, but when there is a heavy case on the wire and it suddenly drops a couple of inches, it throws considerable strain on it. Something could part. As I said, some of the things that went on down below were very serious, but we always looked at it in a different light: 'So what? The insurance are paying and they're the biggest robbers ...' But some bosses seemed to think the money would be coming out of their pockets the way they worried about it. They would scream and blame everybody but themselves. Like the time a black Rolls-Royce was being winched aboard a Brock ship sometime in 1964. It belonged to Laurence Harvey, the actor; it was on its way to North Africa where he was making a movie. The up and down had done his part and the yard-arm man started to heave it in. But the up and down wasn't high enough so the Rolls slammed into the ship's side causing a lot of damage. There was murder over that little incident, but what could be done about it? Nothing. I suppose there were a few snide comments like 'Fuck it, he can afford another one …' I remember another Rolls going to its owner somewhere in Africa, the radio cassette player was whizzed right away, the cigar lighter from the dashboard, the clock.

Mind you, no wonder there were accidents concerning the cargo, some of the ground we had to work over was extremely dangerous. You could have all sorts of uneven cases under your feet and slabs placed across them in all sorts of positions. You had to watch where you walked all the time because if you didn't you could end up with a broken leg or arm. Not to mention other parts of your anatomy. I've had a few falls myself and been very lucky. I have had some close calls and it still shakes you up but you get over it and get on with it. It's not exactly like a dance floor down below. It could look like a Korean landscape sometimes. If you were lucky, for example if there were 40-gallon drums all the same height and with wood placed down on top of these, you had it a lot easier. Then you could push the cars into the corner quite easily but you still had to be careful. There were still pitfalls everywhere. If your mate fell through a hole and went flying, you would immediately say to him, 'Get up, you lazy bastard. Stop lying down on the job …' His shins would be all bruised and bleeding and all you would do was take the piss. You had to take it all. Someone else would probably say, 'Get up, ya fuckin' baby, it's fuckall that …' When you get the car in the wings after you've pushed it there, with one man driving, it has still to be lifted bodily and literally thrown in place. Very rare there was any petrol in the tank because it's all siphoned out on the quay. But if there is a little bit left in the tank, one of us would drive it in place. That's OK if you have a licence but now and again you would get a volunteer who did not have a licence but fancied his chances behind the wheel. I have seen cars driven into the ship's side and smashed. Some ended up down a hole and would have to be heaved out with the fall. Jesus Christ, the damage that was caused. I would have hated to see their faces at the other end. I can imagine what went through their minds. But as I have said, most of the men I worked with took a pride in their work and were very conscientious about it. But accidents would happen. Sometimes we got very heavy lorries and these had to be heaved in because there was no way we could lift these about. If it was a bad job, the eight men would stay on until it got easier. But not always. It was extremely difficult trying to get cars into the wings with just three men, because one man would have to steer it. And if you had any glassbacks with you, that made it all the worse. You all had to pull your weight in these circumstances. I heard about a large boiler that had been loaded here in Birkenhead using a number of strategically placed blocks and it was a work of art the way it was done. It just slotted in like a piece of a jigsaw – only snag was when it arrived in India they couldn't get it out so back it came with a representative to learn how.

Having said all that and despite the good workmanship of the Merseyside docker, I would still prefer the Japanese way. If I had to send anything abroad, it would have to be by these people. I have seen the extra care they take in cargo handling. They have a man down below to make sure nothing is damaged. I remember a case getting damaged on a Japanese ship I was working on, and the man nearly had a fit when he saw it. He had it sent straight out to be repaired. As usual, we said, 'Fuckin' leave it. It's alright …' but he wouldn't have it. I thought then, 'How nice.' And they made sure the hold was clean and free from vermin. Nothing was any bother to them; they were right on the ball.

I am talking now of the days when it was all manhandled – everything, big or small. No such problem now with all the containerisation. Absolutely no skill required to drop these huge things into place, shackle them up and then take the pin out and replace it … hard work. Certainly done a lot of men out of work. But that's progress I suppose, and there isn't anything anyone can do about it.

§

If ever a case came in the hatch that looked interesting I would always have a look just to satisfy my curiosity. You could open a case sometimes without causing too much damage, and you could even put the nails back in the exact place they came from. And some men would open anything. Such a thing happened one day at the Clan when a barrel came in to be stowed among the cargo. You would get the odd thing now and again and you did your best to fit it in somewhere even if it didn't conform. Well, when this barrel came in, they thought it was a gift from Heaven. So right away it is put to one side out of the way so no one can see it. It was soon opened and found to contain some kind of strong alcohol and all hands were throwing it down like there was no tomorrow. Cups and plastic containers were found quickly and everyone was very happy. It wasn't until much later that the barrel, which was destined for some Maharaja in India, was discovered to be some kind of preservative. What really upset them was inside the barrel was a dead monkey which had been his favourite. Luckily, there were no fatalities from this episode. How many times have you heard the expression 'Some men would drink anything'?

§

A moment ago, I was talking about the conditions down below and the ground you had to work on – that is, slabs of timber that were placed to enable you to have some sort of walking way over bad ground. One of the great characters on Birkenhead side was a diminutive man who, to look at, you would definitely say would not set a mouse trap off. He must have weighed in a flyweight. Unshaven, cap askew, no teeth, sallow complexion. This then was 'Slabs' Gandhi. When he sang out to the hatch boss for a sling of slabs, that was it. They would be duly sent in and landed and the wire heaved out. Slabs would inspect the timber like a buyer in an antique shop. He would sort out the best planks and set about laying a deck for the lads. I will exaggerate slightly here but when he had finished it looked like a dance floor! But he wouldn't be satisfied with this – he would ask for more slabs. The hatch boss would say he'd had plenty, but Slabs would snarl up at him and come back with 'I'll fuckin' well tell you when I've got enough; we need more slabs right away …' and we would encourage Slabs all the way. 'Tell him to fuckin' well get more slabs or we're getting' up the ladder …' Slabs would be foaming at the mouth by now, muttering all the time. 'The fuckin' rubbish they sent in is no fuckin' use. It's all rotten and too narrow. Tight bastard won't do fuckall for anyone.' Most times Slabs got his own way and peace reigned for a while. But he certainly was a good man laying down timber. One of his greatest moments came in the Amenity Block during a heated discussion on better working conditions between the Management and the shop stewards. Working off a rig was one of the items debated, and this was a dangerous job. The steward present was Billy 'The Weeping Madonna', and he asked the men if they had any suggestions. Up went Slabs' hand and he stepped forward and said, 'Yeah, give us ten thousand ton of steel and we'll show you how to make money …' Now, this statement had nothing to do with the argument, but the packed hall erupted with applause and the meeting broke up in uproar. They clapped and cheered Slabs and wanted to vote him as a new shop steward. They had to abandon the meeting after that.

§

The Barn Owl was always pulling faces in a peculiar manner and blinking his eyes. His face reminded you of an owl. He was working down below unloading pallet boards and at the same time eating a bar of chocolate. He placed it down on a board while he was working and the board was taken ashore by the deckhand. He missed the chocolate right away and climbed up the ladder to the deck and looked over the rail onto the quay. He saw the stage-end man chewing away and obviously enjoying whatever it was. The Owl shouted down to him, 'Is that my chocolate you're eating?' The stage-end man just shook his head and kept on eating ...

§

Buttons was working down below on the *Clan MacIndoe* sometime in the early Sixties with some other men. They were discharging 40-gallon drums. There weren't any markings on the drums, so they had no idea what they contained. Until one was damaged and started emitting clouds of white powder. Soon everyone was coughing and spluttering and they decided to vacate the deep-tank they were working in. They stood about on the main deck getting some fresh air. They saw the Manager and a ship's officer in a muddle. Then they were told not to go back down the hold, so the lads just stood around talking and taking it easy. Thirty minutes later another gang appeared complete with protective clothing, gasmasks and gloves. Naturally, the lads started asking questions. It transpired the drums were some sort of nuclear waste. This was just one of many examples of dockers loading dangerous cargo in total ignorance. If you saw a skull and crossbones, naturally you would treat it with respect. It took an accident for these incidents to be found out.

I have already mentioned about the docker who could have been severely burned in a very private place simply because the ship he was working on wasn't maintained properly and, as a result, a valve couldn't be turned because of rust. The water would have relieved his agony.

Trouble would start if we asked for a few shilling extra for working such cargo. It would be flatly refused, or a few pennies would be offered. This was like adding insult to injury. So we would leave the ship until our demands were met. This would be one of the reasons the public got the wrong idea about the so-called lazy dockers.

One time when Billy S., Jimmy S. and Lucky were working together, Billy worked a fast one on one of the watchmen. He threw a case of cigarettes from the tween deck into the lower hold, but the watchman saw him and asked for them to be returned promptly or he would inform the police. They had no choice but to do as he asked.

Also in the tween deck was a spare propeller for the ship, which was a common practice by ship owners. The boys came back after dinner and caught the watchman pulling his trousers up from behind the propeller. Men used to urinate in a corner rather than go ashore, which took some time, but this watchman had defecated and the smell was horrendous. Naturally, the boys were horrified and Billy made quite a scene, and threatened to call the ship's boss. The word strike was mentioned a few times unless the cigarettes were made available. They had the watchman, who by now was terrified, over a barrel. He had no choice but to let them help themselves.

§

Me, Man with No Arms, Friday Frank and a few others were down No. 2 on a City boat at North Quay. I remember it well. Shirts, dressing gowns, shoes, boots, all on the last day of loading, so it was a bit of a rush. Opened another case that was underneath some tractors. Bingo. Full of leather zip-up jackets. With side pockets. All black. I got four for myself. There were shirts all over the place – the lads had made a mess. And what was worse, someone had shit among them. The smell was overpowering. I knew who had done it, but couldn't understand why he had to do it in that particular place. Also, why the hell didn't they have a watchman down that hatch? Their loss.

§

I was on the mini shift at the Clan with Godfrey C. and a couple of Easter Bunnies. We were landing a very heavy type of steel wheels under our feet. They were coming in one at a time on a short rope with three steel clamps under the rim all spread out. We had landed one but wanted it picked up again so we could place it properly. The deckhand was asked to take the weight and this he did, but unfortunately one of the grabs flew off and hit me in the chest. It was like being hit with a sledgehammer, and I fell over, the wind knocked completely out of me. I couldn't inhale properly and was desperately trying to get my breath. I could hear Godfrey screaming at the Bunnies to help me, but there was nothing they could have done anyway. I have heard the expression kicked like a mule, but actually that was what it was like. I was relieved to start breathing normally. When those dogs fly off, you could easily lose an eye or several teeth.

§

Down below one time with the Angry Cat, the Leper, Rock Ferry Donkey and Ray the Liar, we were working across the hatch with small but very heavy cases, so heavy it took two of us to turn them over using our hooks. We did one or two longers across the hatch and then Mr Magoo, the hatch boss, shouted down, 'Sending in some heavier cases to go on top of those, OK?'

Right away, the lads start screaming for a stacker …

'Calm down,' says Mr Magoo. 'I'm sending one in, OK? While you're waiting for it, just rest your weary bodies …'

'Sarcastic prick,' said the Angry Cat. 'As soon as the job gets going, he'll be sitting in the Poulton Vics getting pissed.'

'Jealous, are we?' said Ray.

'Stand in below,' shouted the deckhand, 'stacker coming over …'

We all stood in under the protection of the lower tween deck while it was lowered. Once it was down we unscrewed the four shackles and let the fall go ashore. Then we all sat around while waiting for the huge battery to be sent in. Suddenly, there was the sound of splintering wood and there was the Fugitive attacking one of the small cases. 'Don't know why you're doing that,' said the Leper. 'Can't be anything worth taking out. Probably steel or iron parts for some job out in Beira, going by the fuckin' weight.'

'Well, if it's full of gold watches, you won't want any, will you?'

'No fuckin' chance,' said the Leper.

It turned out it was steel bars about 18 inches long, highly polished. No wonder they were heavy. For a special piece of machinery. Definitely need steel toecaps for some of the stuff we handled.

'Here comes the battery,' someone said. We lowered it onto the stacker, unshackled it and sent it ashore.

The driver shouted down, 'Oright if I go for a bevy, lads? Won't be long. Loads of cases comin' in.'

We could all handle a stacker no bother.

'Yeah. Go on. Fuck off,' shouted the Cat

'Right,' asked the Leper, 'who's going to drive the stacker?'

The Fugitive volunteered. 'Where's me gloves before I get started?' he asked.

'You and your fuckin' gloves. Scared of getting our hands dirty, are we?' sneered the Cat.

'No. What would my wife say if my hands were rough?'

'She never complained to me,' sniggered Ray.

The Donkey spoke up: 'That's bad gear saying that.'

Another ship another time. Down below on a Harrison boat. Friday Frank, Harry Worth, Jimmy, Harry the Birdman, and myself. Boss shouted down, 'Sending in a stacker, lads. Lengths of steel rod. Go right across the hatch. Make sure there's plenty of deals separating them, OK?'

'We ain't got none down here, so you'd better get some sent down before the deckhands start giving us a hard time,' shouted Harry Worth.

'You tell him, Harry,' said Friday Frank. The stacker driver was seen climbing down the ladder.

'It's Doctor Beaker,' said Harry, still holding a book in his hand.

'Put your fuckin' book away and get some of your fuckin' fingers around the shackles when we land it.'

Slowly, the deckhand landed it and slackened the fall. The shackles were released, pins screwed back in and held away from the stacker as the deckhand took the fall up.

Going off the ship the next morning, Jimmy offered the lads a lift as he passed close by where they lived. They very nearly didn't make it, because Jimmy hit the kerb and knocked a lamp post down. They were all shaken up and went on their way. They could hear Jimmy laughing.

The following night, we carried on where the day workers had finished. They had left some small cases in the wings and were to get some cartons to go on top right up to the deck-head. While we were waiting for the first sling to come in, we were taking the piss out of Jimmy. We were having a good laugh about what happened when he nearly wiped out the lads in the back of his van. He was taking some stick but he started laughing. Nothing upset him. 'You didn't complain when I offered you all a lift.'

'Yeah, you crazy fucker. Nearly put us in hospital or the fuckin' mortuary,' said Harry the Birdman. 'Never been so fuckin' scared in my life.'

'What happened to the van, Jimmy?' asked the Fugitive.

Had to scrap it this afternoon. The steering was damaged when I hit the kerb. Would have cost too much to get it fixed. The van only cost me a hundred. So I'm going to take some lessons and I'll get another van later.'

'What lessons, Jimmy?' asked the Fugitive. 'Driving lessons, of course,' replied Jimmy.

'You mean to say you don't have a driving licence?' asked Harry.

'Have I fuck,' replied Jimmy, laughing.

'That means you don't have insurance?'

'No. I do have a provisional licence though.'

Suddenly they heard the sound of splintering wood and saw the Fugitive attacking one of the wooden cases with the bar.

'He never gives up, does he?' said the Suitcase.

They all strolled over to have a look. The metal bands had been snapped off and the wood ripped apart. The Fugitive reached in and pulled out a small heavy object wrapped in grease-proof paper. It was a carpenter's wood plane. The case was full of tools. Planes, ratchet screwdrivers, pliers, saws, metal tape, measures, spirit levels.

'Anyone want any of this stuff?' asked the Fugitive.

'I'll have a couple of screwdrivers,' said Harry. 'Those planes are too bulky.'

'Anyone else?' asked the Fugitive. 'Don't want anyone saying I'm greedy.' Nobody else was interested. 'OK if I go ashore and look for some sacks strong enough to put some of these in? They will fit nicely in my book. Give me fifteen minutes to sort something out.'

He was back in twenty minutes.

'Saw the lads on the quay. They're gonna land my stuff and stash it somewhere out the way until we leave the ship. I'll be letting them have some tools just to keep them sweet. Mickey M. is on the quay. He will do a good job and let us know if any of the boys are sniffing around. If it's all clear, I'll fill my boot up. Anyone need a lift, you're welcome, but anyone on the gate, I won't be stopping.'

Everyone declined. The Fugitive laughed. He started filling some thick sack he found in the shed. They were put in the next sling to go ashore and Mickey did the necessary.

The deckhands knew what was going on, but were not bothered, and what they didn't know wouldn't hurt them. Most deckhands were OK and were not averse to anything that was going, especially the hard stuff. Wintertime they had it rough sitting behind a winch in a biting wind and hailstones. Some would build some kind of shelter, improvised of course. They were a great bunch of men.

§

Case came in one day at the Clan containing hair clippers. The type the barber used to use. Right away some knowall tells you you can't get rid of them. But I never believed anyone anyway. So I filled my pockets and stuffed some down my shirt. In those days I used to wear an ex-army combat jacket with hundreds of burglar-type pockets. I left the hatch and got onto the main deck and made my way to the gangway. As I was going down towards the quay, who should be coming up the gangway but a policeman! I did feel rather bulky but I just couldn't turn around – that would have been a dead giveaway. So I carried on. As we passed each other I heard a clatter as a few clippers fell out of a hole in my pocket. He was in a hurry and didn't seem to hear anything. Mind you, there was plenty of noise to cover that sort of thing, what with all the winches going and men shouting. I kept going, leaving them where they had fallen – too bad.

A similar incident occurred some time later. Got some made-up gear down the hatch – kiddies clothes. We were working in the square of the hatch at that time and the ship was on the finish. The quay hands were sending some metal rods in, like conduit pipes. We were working the welt and while the other gang were working we were getting dressed ready to go off. I was like Billy Bunter with all the gear on and so were the others. We had that much on us we could hardly bend over. Just as we were about to leave the hatch, a sling fell on Jerry, and he was thrown to the ground pinned by his legs. It was completely unexpected and we couldn't do much because we could hardly move being dressed up. But we did what we could. Jerry wasn't too badly hurt, nothing broken. So we had to leave him. We apologised to him of course, and we left with his voice ringing in our ears: 'You lousy fuckin' bastards ... you pricks ...' We could hardly move for laughing, but we had to get off before the police came. They always do when an accident happens. Halfway down the gangway I was met by another policeman. He could hardly get past me. I got a few more grey hairs. I had still to get on my scooter and get out the gate ... but all went well. Never did like getting dressed up with gear like that or cloth. Come to that, never liked carrying whisky. But what can you do when you want to earn a few shillings? A few years later we used to take twenty ton on a motor or fill a large van up. Jerry was only joking anyway; he knew we couldn't help him and he wasn't in any great danger. But we had many a laugh over it. The very idea of us leaving him to bleed to death because we were carrying. But you had to have a sense of humour, and the docker had the greatest in the world.

§

A lot of expertise and skill combined is used to get these large cases out of the way. Wheel blocks and wires have to be used. These have got to be positioned in just the right place to be of any use. The higher the better up on the ship's side. But many was the time you won't find a suitable ringbolt welded into the deck-head or the ships side. In that case you have to improvise as best you can. So you get a gall wire. This is usually about four feet long with an eye splice at each end. With a bit of luck you might find a small aperture up on the deck-head and you then try and get the end through. This can be extremely difficult with one leg crooked over a stringer, trying to keep your balance. Once you have got the wire in place, you then have to secure the block to the two eyes with a shackle. Then someone will pass you the runner wire from the winch, which has to be locked in position ready for heaving. All this takes place high up the ship's side, maybe twenty feet or more. Officially, wooden ladders are supposed to be used, but very rarely did I see one being used. Most of the lads climbed up the stringers like monkeys with a block in their hands. The blocks were about twenty pounds in weight, so it was praiseworthy of the men to carry out these tasks with never a murmur of complaint. Of course, we swore and turned the air blue with the most foul language imaginable, but it was all in the best humour possible.

The Angel (to the man above him holding the block): 'Watch you don't drop that fuckin' thing on my head …'

The Mole: 'Don't be fuckin' worryin' … wouldn't make any difference, would it?'

The Angel: 'I am fuckin' worried … we should have a ladder here. You wouldn't get a light if you fell.'

The Mole: 'Well, it's too late now. Anyway, you know how long it takes them to find a ladder? We could have the job finished before then, couldn't we?'

The Angel: 'I suppose so. But remember the Grey Rat? He fell and broke his fuckin' legs … Jesus! The fuckin' screams out of him when they were takin' him out in the tub …'

The Mole: 'That was because the deckhand took the weight on the yard too soon and banged against the coaming …'

The Angel: 'Yeah, the prick was full of whisky and thought it was fuckin' hilarious … the poor Rat was off for three months with both legs in plaster and got told off for his pains. Anyway, I thought rats were supposed to be nimble? We've seen them run along the stringers and jump down, but not Grey Rats, must be a different species …'

They both broke up laughing.

§

Lovely Husband was always saying how good he was to his wife. Our Lady of Sorrows was always complaining about something or other. Lonely Baker was quoted as saying, 'There's only me and me tart.' Tween deck Jimmy always seemed to be in the tween deck looking for wood to throw down, and then he would take hours to come down into the lower hold in case there was any work. Flock Head, otherwise known as Jimmy M., had a head like a burst mattress. The Baldy Cat was always saying he didn't have the fare (fur) when he boarded the bus. The Laughing Skull was a hatch boss. Bacon for Berty was the ship's boss at the Clan and used to be a butcher. Electric Whiskers was a deckhand. Billy the Fish was a crane driver. Good Shepherd (J.C.) was a ship's boss and saved two cows (women) from the dock when they fell in; they had been aboard the ship entertaining some of the crew. Rosy Apples was Billy E. Len the Bobby was an ex-policeman. Pontius Pilot was always washing his hands. Contented Diner was always saying, 'I've got enough on my plate.' Bird Doctor would say, 'This lark's no good.' Sheriff, another hatch boss, would be saying, 'What's the holdup, lads?' Rattler, named due to his false teeth rattling. The Surgeon was always saying, 'Now then, cut that out.' The Auctioneer was a bogey driver and would knock anyone down. Piano – 'I think the men play on me.' Teddy P. was The Wicked Uncle. Acid Drop was never seen to smile. Bacon Bones used to work in a butcher's shop. The Hawk was a docker with hawk-like features. Chicken Rustler would walk out the gate with frozen chickens under his coat. Eternal Youth never seemed to get any older. The Zombie looked like the walking dead. Vampire was a dead ringer for Bela Lugosi. Grumpy was always moaning. The Owl would say, 'Is me owl feller down there?' His father worked down below in the hold.

There was a docker called Green Fingers who hit on a brilliant idea. He was a good bagman. In his spare time he was a keen gardener, and would be found most weekends at his allotment. It was whilst digging that he hit upon his idea of burying his loot, and marking the place with a bamboo cane. When the police searched his house on the odd occasion they never could find any evidence.

Slow-talking Joney would stop anyone who was unfortunate enough to meet him. He would take hours telling you all his woes. Then when you could get a word in and start to tell him something, he would reply, 'Fuck off, don't tell me your troubles.'

The Magician said he was a member of the famous Circle, but nobody believed him. Everyone thought he was a weirdo. Most dockers wished he would disappear off the face of the earth.

Doctor Beaker was a crane driver who bore a striking resemblance to the cartoon character on television. The Mortician was a man who looked like he was about to do an autopsy on you.

The Toff had airs and graces and was always boasting about eating his meals in a huge dining room. Candelabra, silver cutlery, wine, etc., but one of the lads knew him and told us he was a liar. It came about because one of the lads did a bit of private hire at the week and was given the Toff's address and went there to pick someone up. But when he arrived, he didn't hang around because it looked like a derelict house. But it was the correct address.

§

Big Arthur S. wanted to go for a drink but was skint. Someone offered him his entrance fee if he would dive in the dock and swim across, from the Clan to the China berth, which was about two hundred yards or so. So Big Arthur dived in straight away and swam across and got out the other side. He was given his money, and it was getting on for winter too.

§

Big A. and Sammy M. were working together with some others down below, who were loading railway sleepers. These were made of metal and very awkward to handle. They were usually about 6 feet long and bound with steel bands to hold them together. I used to hate them. They would come into the hatch on two wire slings. If it happened to be raining, it was made all the more dangerous because you would be slipping and sliding all over the place. Trying to keep your feet and trying to stow the sleepers was an ordeal. One sling came in and burst and they all came adrift. Everyone scattered but Big A. was unlucky. He was clipped on the ankle and went down. Harry C. was the hatch boss and he shouted down, 'Don't move him. I'll send a tub in.' The tub was dragged out from under a load of dunnage, and it was filthy and full of debris as usual. By this time the lads were looking for a nice piece of wood to use as a splint because they thought his leg was broken. This is where the fun started. The splint was greenheart, a very heavy wood used for making piers, plus it was over six feet long and the tub was only about four feet long. So they couldn't get him in the tub. There were red faces all round. Some men just broke up but it wasn't so funny for Big A.

§

Jacko, otherwise known as the Screaming Skull, and Billy B. were down below at Bromborough Dock working on a ship discharging peanuts. It was their first day on the docks actually. Working with them was a man of about forty who said he had been jilted at the age of nineteen. During the course of the conversion, it got around to sex. They asked the man how did he manage for female company and nooky. There was a good deal of banter going on and as usual someone spoilt it by going too far. The man resented the implied suggestion that he tore the head off it (masturbated), and he went for Jacko, who flattened him right away.

Another time in the same dock the same men were working with some of the local labourers. Among them were a father and his two sons. During the afternoon, the father collapsed in a heap. His two sons were shouting up to the deckhand to get an ambulance. But Jacko had checked the man and came to the conclusion that he was dead, and shouted out, 'Don't bother with the ambulance, get the undertaker, he's snuffed it.' This didn't go down very well with the other men. But that's the way it was on the docks.

The Skull, Jacko and Billy B. were sent to Ellesmere Port docks once after signing all week and were not too happy about it. It meant they were about to work for practically nothing after signing the book. So all week they duly set off for Ellesmere Port and when they arrived the first place they would look for was the dock's canteen. For some reason it was closed, and this did not make them any happier. Jack H. was in their gang, and he was elected spokesman. The management tried to get them to start work right away, but to no avail. So a bigger wheel was sent for to try and diffuse the situation. This man had to come from Manchester docks. He was told by Jacko in no uncertain terms that 'we are not starting without toast in our tummies'.

§

Here are a few more nicknames. Johnny 'What's the lady having?' Finn. George was 'Fuck Fuck'. Alf D. was known as Gary Glitter – 'Wanna be in my gang?' George Davies was a footballer, and would say, 'Watch my legs.' Wedding Cake got married and brought some cake in for the lads. Harbour Master knew all the ship's movements, when it was due in, how long, what cargo. Nutnose, otherwise known as Russell, was a ship's boss. Spread the Net was another ship's boss (Smith's).

The Cockroach was on the back of a lorry with some other Liverpool dockers getting a lift. They were all merry after drinking whisky down below, and the Cockroach fell off going out of the gate, he landed on his back, arms and legs up in the air, and someone said, 'Look at the cockroach.'

The Vegetarian wouldn't go near the meat ships. Broken Bulb would say, 'Won't get a light out of this one ...' Hovis was always browned off. Cassius Clay said, 'Where's the gloves?' With London Fog, the fog never lifted. The Ghost was always moaning. Dr Jekyll was always saying, 'I need a change.' Sell the bed was always on nights. The Jelly said, 'One more night and I'll be set.' The Coward had holes in the back of his coat. Stanley Matthews said, 'I'll take this corner.' Sad Tales was always glum. Six on the Floor was a holdsman with six children. Gay Pierre was a deckhand.

Dr Feelgood said, 'How are we lads? All OK? I feel great myself. Right, come on then, let's get stuck in.' Lord Tapper was always asking for a loan. Flash Kid was always smartly dressed. Slipaway was always first away from the job. Can and Cups was always making the tea, and was also known as High Priest of Nights. The Angry Cat always snarling at something or other. Cow and Gate was told where the whisky was but took some Cow and Gate instead. Undertaker used to say, 'We'll bury this case.' The Echo said, 'It's news to me ...' Parish Priest only worked on a Sunday. Olympic Torch never went out.

§

Deadlegs was walking out the gate with a bottle of whisky hidden under his coat. Just as he drew level with the Policeman, the bottle fell and smashed on the floor. Deadlegs was all alone but he looked everywhere, even up in the air, as if the bottle had arrived anywhere but from him. The Policeman came over, looking very serious. Before he could open his mouth, Deadlegs jumped in with, 'Where did that come from?' Of course, the Policeman suggested it had fallen from beneath his coat. 'Don't know nothing about it,' replied Deadlegs indignantly. The Policeman really couldn't do anything about the situation because there was no evidence. Grudgingly, he had to let Deadlegs go.

Charley P. got grabbed at the gate and searched. He was taking a chance with some loose tea he had taken from down below. It was found and he was arrested. He was fined five pounds and warned of the perils of pilfering. From then on he was known as the Tea Leaf (thief).

§

Our last job was taking 30 tons of sheet steel from the docks to Queensferry to our contact to supervise our steel being transferred onto another vehicle. But here everything went wrong. Our contact failed to appear. If we had known, we could easily have taken the steel back to the docks; no one would have been the wiser. We left and hoped the contact would appear and get it sorted. He never arrived.

Two days later, we were arrested. We were on bail for nine months before we appeared at the Liverpool Crown Court where we were found guilty and sentenced to three years. The worst thing in the world is to have your liberty taken away.

In the stockade in Egypt we lived under canvas surrounded by barbed wire and were not allowed to talk. Everything was done on the double. You had to ask for permission to speak to one of the Staff Sergeants. We had to run and climb over an assault course every day. It did not bother me one iota. We were out in nice, sunny weather. But a closed prison was completely the opposite. Banged up for twenty-three hours except when you were allowed out to go and get your food on a tray and get back to your cell. That is when the reality hits home. Bodily functions in a bucket. Two other men in the same cell. People shouting, keys jangling, doors slamming. Sometimes inmates screaming. Three men hanged themselves while I was in Strangeways prison in Manchester. This was certainly a cultural shock to me. Surrounded by career criminals, druggies, car thieves, burglars, drunks, people who could not read or write. Many were repeat offenders. Some thought I was from another planet because I was so naive.

After four months in a closed prison I was sent to an open prison. To me, it was Paradise. Army-style billets. privacy, library, football field, a pond if you wanted to fish. You could walk out the main gate if you wanted to, but if you were caught, you were sent back to a closed prison. Some did. They thought I was crazy because I was so happy to walk around in the pouring rain. After eight months in that holiday camp I was released on parole for twelve months. It was a part of my life I could have done without.

§

I live near Birkenhead docks and drive past nearly every day. Duke Street bridge and the Four Bridges. The Sixties would see the Alfred Basin full of ships waiting to come through to the West Float, maybe two ships loading at the Black sheds. Into the West Float, Blue Funnel berths on the left, Clan sheds nearby. Opposite the Clan were the Mills waiting for the grain. Further up through Duke Street and Rea's Wharf on the left, they handled coal and scrap. Opposite was the Golden Mile, which took all the City and the Harrisons and went right up to the Bidston Dock. The Bidston Dock could hold two or three ships. This was filled in years ago and the swing bridge fixed permanently in place for road traffic. Now and then I drive around the dock estate to visit the odd ship that may call in. I drive down the Clan quays and park up. Gone were the magnificent Blue Funnel ships with illustrious name from Greek mythology: *Perseus, Jason, Achilles, Hector, Peleus*. At the time of writing, there are two Everard tankers and two ex-Royal Navy vessels laid up.

When I think of the ships that graced these wharves and quays: gone forever never to be seen ever again. Ellerman, Clan, Scindia Steam, Brocklebank, T&J Harrison, Safmarine, Japanese Maru, Haynes, even the odd tramp would call in to discharge a few ton or a load. Like the *Whitehorse*, a Second World War Liberty steamer, ex-*Marabank*. She discharged about 30 tons of asbestos. Then there were the tramps that called with grain for Uveco or Ranks. Others picked up tons of scrap from Rea's and went to Japan and the whole lot was scrapped, even the ship. Flags of Panama, Somalia, Honduras, Greece, Turkey, Lebanon, Malta, Cyprus. I remember a tramp from Cambodia. Names that stick in my memory like *White Eagle, Heracles, Sideris, Patapsco River, Maria Lemos, Kyra, Stella Azura, Maria Stathatos, Maria De Lourdes, Ramon De Larrinaga*, and many more, too numerous to mention here. It was exciting for me every day to walk up a ship's gangway and step onto the main deck.

In the West Float in a corner near Duke Street bridge are two former ferry boats laid up. Another sign of the times. Just behind them, tied up at a deserted jetty, is a Second World War LST, still in wartime grey paint. It used to be a club in Liverpool called Landfall. Another ship that stands out in my memory in Birkenhead was a tramp called *Zinnia*, who came here several times – red funnel, black top, and a white stag on the funnel.

I see another famous Mersey landmark has left for Sweden – the huge floating crane *Mammoth*. Hard to believe she was sixty years old. She earned her place in Mersey maritime history. I always wanted to climb to the top of her jib to take some photos, but I don't think I would have been given permission somehow. Anyway, it's too late now.

Two or three City or Ellerman ships could be seen here in the 1960s. Now Birkenhead docks are quiet and still.

Ghosts

As I leaned on the rail of Duke Street bridge, with my shoulder wet with rain, looking around the deserted quays, I knew things will never be the same.

From where I stand I can see the sheds of the China and the Clan, and I think of the laughs I had down here when I was a younger man.

I idly watch a fisherman tending to his net, and my mind wandered back to some of the characters I have met.

There's Dickie Rudd and Danny Campbell in competition they would sing, and the Penguin and the Cat laying down a sling.

Here's the Wet Dog and the Owl, even Itchy Mick, the Dandy Docker and Flipper, and the Day-old Chick.

I've watched the Woodchurch Hillbillies working with the Crow, with Head Em Up, Red Evan and the Lemon Drop below.

In the shed the Miner's Lamp with the Undertaker, on the other Fill the Cot and the Lonely Baker.

Cowboy Jones and Mister Wonderful are working with a friend, and the Duke is in the Rapier running to the old stage end.

The Baron and Jed Clampitt are driving quayside cranes, and down below Red Riding Hood, the Sick Lobster and Hercules unchained.

The Red Terror and the White Hunter each had a secret wish, to be on the opposite side to the Moreton Donkey and the Reluctant Fish.

From my lofty perch above the quay I watch this tale unfold, of Paddy the Pig and the Milky Bar Kid, the Talking Balloon in the hold.

I know I haven't got all the names and I say this with a sigh, for most of the names that you read here are welting in the sky.

The sound of a car horn entered my thoughts and woke me from my dream, and I found that I was once again part of a deserted scene.

When I looked all around me with no signs of a mast, I realised that I'd journeyed well into the past.

As I walked away from the bridge, my heart was heavy with pain, and I found my face was wet but it was just rain.

The nicknames of the above are all true; but they only worked together for the purpose of this poem.

ALSO AVAILABLE FROM AMBERLEY PUBLISHING

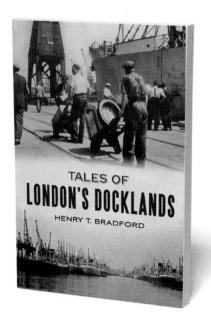

Tales of London's Docklands
Henry T. Bradford

An engaging and endearing account of the day-to-day experiences of hardworking dockers in the Port of London after the Second World War. These real-life stories highlight the harshness, brutality and poverty experienced during the author's time spent working in the dock industry. Yet they also capture the humour and camaraderie that existed among the dockers, revealing the characters that shined through the backbreaking and dangerous daily toil.

ISBN 978-1-4456-0166-3
Paperback   96 pages   £10.99

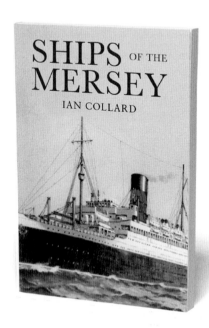

Ships of the Mersey:
A Photographic History
Ian Collard

Ian Collard brings together a superb selection of images of shipping on the river from the 1860s to the present day, looking at how the ports on either side of the river have developed and the ships which have called there.

From the Mersey ferries to the greatest of ocean liners, *Ships of the Mersey* tells the story of the ships, the people and the buildings of the Mersey docks system.

ISBN 978-184868-058-6
Paperback   128 pages   £12.99

www.amberleybooks.com